THE COMPLETE GUIDE TO BOERBOELS

Desirée Botha

Publication Data

Desirée Botha

The Complete Guide to Boerboels – First edition.

Summary: "Successfully raising a Boerboel dog from puppy to old age" – Provided by publisher.

ISBN: 978-1-954288-46-1

[1. Boerboels – Non-Fiction] I. Title.

This book has been written with the published intent to provide accurate and author-itative information in regard to the subject matter included. While every reasonable precaution has been taken in preparation of this book the author and publisher expressly disclaim responsibility for any errors, omissions, or adverse effects arising from the use or application of the information contained inside. The techniques and suggestions are to be used at the reader's discretion and are not to be considered a substitute for professional veterinary care. If you suspect a medical problem with your dog, consult your veterinarian.

Design by Sorin Rădulescu
First paperback edition, 2022

TABLE OF CONTENTS

INTRODUCTION

I have had a lot of experience loving and caring for the Boerboel breed. Furthermore, I am someone who really wants all new dog parents and their puppies to have the best experience that they can have.

I have had Boerboels since I was two years old. The last Boerboel I had died a few years ago when I was 29. That is a lot of time spent loving dogs of one breed and caring for them. I know what makes this breed truly unique. I have seen how different each dog can be, and I know the difficulties that any prospective Boerboel owner can face if they don't know the breed as well as I do. So, while I am not a vet or a professional dog trainer, I do have a lot of insights that could help a new dog parent when getting ready for a new dog.

A dog should be with its family its whole life. To help to make that goal easier, I will share the knowledge that I have gained with you. Hopefully, that knowledge and some of the tricks that I have learned can help you on your journey with your own dog.

These big, beautiful balls of fur can be loving, caring, and incredibly loyal. But they can also be fiercely protective, sometimes even too protective, and incredibly stubborn and set in their ways. Hopefully, this book will help new owners know what to expect so that the experience with your new pup can be wonderful for both of you.

CHAPTER 1
History of Boerboels

This giant Mastiff dog has a long, rich history in South Africa. Their origins can be traced back to the 1800s when the first settlers created towns where ships could dock and restock in the southernmost part of Africa. Many of these settlers were moving to South Africa permanently, so their families and their pets came with them.

Photo Courtesy
of Danielle Radey
Mae Boerboels

Mae Boerboel
THE EYES OF AFRICA

Photo Courtesy
of Ekaterina Shimoliuk

The Dutch East India Company sent Jan Van Riebeeck to establish the first trading post in the area that we now know as Cape Town, South Africa. With him came a big, strong Mastiff-type breed that the history books call a Bullenbijter, or bull biter. Many of the colonists who traveled with Riebeeck or after him also brought their biggest and strongest Mastiff dogs with them for protection.

Historians believe there were also already big dogs on the continent that belonged to the native African people. These dogs interbred with the dogs of the Europeans and created a Mastiff that was much bigger and stronger. Interestingly, if you look at the historical descriptions of a few different breeds of dogs that were found in Africa at the time, many sound very similar to the Boerboels we know today.

When diamonds were found in South Africa years later, companies like De Beers imported true Bull Mastiffs. The English imported long-legged Bulldogs during the Anglo-Boer War, and again, all of these dogs started to interbreed. Eventually, this interbreeding became the Boerboel breed we know today.

While we don't know exactly what types of breeds make up the Boerboel's full ancestry, we do know these gentle giants are extremely large, super strong, and very fast.

FUN FACT
American Boerboel Club (ABC)

The American Boerboel Club (ABC) was founded in 2006 and is recognized as the breed's parent club by the American Kennel Club (AKC). The ABC provides an approved breeder list for Boerboels and hosts several events throughout the year. For more information about becoming a member or approved breeder, visit the ABC website at www.americanboerboelclub.com.

The Boerboel gets its name from the Afrikaans word "Boer" (farmer) and the word for "Boel" that could just mean "dog" or might be a shortening of the word "boelhond," meaning bulldog. In essence, the name just means "farmer's dog."

Farmers kept Boerboels because the more rural areas of South Africa could be dangerous, and these dogs would protect their humans and the humans' property with their lives. They were also working dogs that herded cattle, and a pack of them could fight off wild animals like leopards and baboons if necessary. As a result, Boerboels have more courage than most dogs, but that isn't always a good thing. Sometimes even when you want them to back down, they won't when it comes to protecting their family.

Physical appearance and variations of a Boerboel

"Boerboels should not be oversized dogs like English Mastiffs. They should not be slow, excessively bulky, or fat, as this is counterproductive to being a working dog. Boerboels should, first and foremost, be able to endure working all day in the heat; they should have drive and stamina. The Boerboel was created for working ability above all else, and in order to keep the breed as it was originally created for, breeders must not look to breed dogs that are oversized or with too much bulk as that will destroy the integrity and true nature of the breed. This is a breed that should always have a free-flowing gait and be at ease on their feet for long periods of time, running, jumping, and working. That's the mark of a TRUE Boerboel."

MICHELLE CONVIS
Adara Ridge Boerboels

Photo Courtesy
of Nico Kilian

There is almost nothing cuter and more beautiful than a Boerboel puppy.

There is a reason that Boerboels are called a giant breed. They are massive. One of my dogs was taller than me when he stood on two paws with his front paws on my shoulders.

Funnily enough, they don't look all that massive when you get them as puppies of about 8 to 10 weeks old. So you need to know that they will grow and grow and grow some more. Full-grown adults will normally weigh anywhere from 110–200 pounds.

Most male Boerboels average 24 to 28 inches in height when measured at the shoulders. Females are a little bit smaller, around 22 to 25 inches in height. The best indication would be to look at the parents' size.

Boerboels have a very distinct look around their face. All of them have black noses, and many of them have a dark spot over their facial area. For some, that dark area can be so big that it completely covers the eyes and face. It can look as if the puppy's face was dipped into a bucket of black paint.

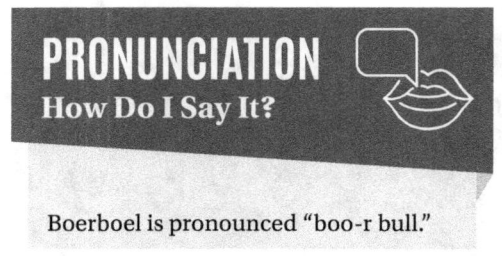

PRONUNCIATION
How Do I Say It?

Boerboel is pronounced "boo-r bull."

Boerboels have short, straight overcoats that should be really shiny and beautiful in a healthy dog, and they also have a soft, dense undercoat. They come in different shades of red, brown, yellow, and brindle. They also sometimes come in black, but it should be noted that this color is still not accepted by many breeders' societies, outside of the South African Boerboel Breeders Society, which is the registered custodian of the breed.

Boerboels have blocky heads and a super-strong bone structure with well-developed muscles. Puppies look stocky, with strong little legs, and they might have some loose excess skin in preparation for all of that growing that they need to do. They are large animals that can still move pretty quickly and quietly.

Because the South African Boerboel Breeders Society is the registered custodian of the breed, they are still the final authority when it comes to breed specifics. But it is good to note the Boerboel societies in your own area and what they expect to see from the breed. In the United Kingdom, the Boerboel Breed Society is the only one with a legal registry. They still work very closely with the SABBS, and they help to import dogs from strong bloodlines in South Africa to be able to breed and create a strong lineage in the UK too. They do DNA profiling, so they are a good resource for finding a really great pup in the UK. At the same time, they adhere to the breed guidelines of the SABBS with the height, weight, and color requirements I have already mentioned.

For the USA, the American Kennel Club (AKC) is the authority on what the breed standard is for your dog to compete. According to the AKC's website, the breed standard for male Boerboels is 24 to 27 inches and 22 to 25 inches for females, with a weight of 150 to 200 pounds. The AKC accepts bridle, brown, cream, red, reddish-brown, and tawny as colors for the Boerboel.

Note that as the AKC has only recognized Boerboels as a breed since 2015, the breed standards might eventually change.

There are also a number of Boerboel clubs in America that could help new dog owners find the best and healthiest puppies. The American Boerboel Club, for example, has a lot of events where you can get together with other Boerboel enthusiasts and share stories, as well as get advice.

Working dogs

Boerboels are incredibly smart dogs that are also naturally dominant. They were originally bred to keep family and/or cattle and land safe, as well as taking down big game while hunting with their owners. So giving them a job is one way of making sure these dogs are happy and fulfilled.

There might be times you see your Boerboel trying to herd your family, rounding everyone up for "protection." This can be really cute at first in a small puppy, but when your pup becomes a big 200-pound dog, it can become less funny. So, it is a behavior that needs to be kept in check right from the start, and you need to make sure that your dog knows you are the one in charge.

Photo Courtesy
of Demetrus Dunbar

That said, Boerboels are gentle dogs that are really great with kids if they are exposed to children from a young age. These days they are used for therapy work and working with kids.

Your responsibility will be to make sure your Boerboel is happy and doesn't get bored. Though they are great family dogs, they need to be stimulated and interacted with. A dog that is bored generally becomes destructive. And a bored dog as large as a Boerboel can result in some serious damage.

Behavioral characteristics

"

"Boerboels are headstrong but intelligent and obedient. They learn fast and are extremely concerned with the approval of their masters. They are amazing guardians and are agile and quick on their feet. Unlike other Mastiff breeds, Boerboels are not lazy couch potatoes. These are true working dogs. They like lots of room to roam and run, and having a sizeable area to move around in ensures they maintain their athletic physique. They are loving and gentle with children and tend to be good with other animals when raised with them. They have a reliable temperament, and when taught something, Boerboels remember it for life."

MICHELLE CONVIS
Adara Ridge Boerboels

"

As we have already mentioned, these dogs are highly intelligent and also incredibly loyal. There is a reason that they are sometimes called Velcro dogs. They want to be close to you and need to be part of the family in order to be truly happy. This very loyalty can create some difficulties later on if Boerboels aren't socialized properly, which we will discuss later in the book.

Boerboels are obedient and eager to please, but if they sense any uncertainty from you, their domineering traits could take over. As such, they might not be the best choice for first-time dog owners, but I believe that any pet parents who really want what is best for their dogs and who are willing to put in the time and the effort of learning the breed's habits can learn how to care for a Boerboel. It might just take a lot of dedication, consistency, and love.

Boerboels don't generally like water; at least, none of mine ever did. So, if you want a dog to go swimming with you, then it might be better to look into a different breed. It is possible to train Boerboels to tolerate water, such as for bath time, but this needs to be done fairly early on in a puppy's life.

Boerboels are stubborn and like to have things their own way. I had one dog that absolutely hated one of our garden ornaments. Every single day we would find it outside the gate. I would put it back into place, and then she would pick it up and throw it over the gate again. Eventually, we just moved the ornament out of her sight.

Photo Courtesy of Monica Sciocatti

If they have enough toys and stimulation, Boerboels aren't generally big diggers. They would rather chew on everything, but again, this can be helped with enough attention and toys. Younger dogs need longer walks to burn off the excess energy. As they get older, you can get away with taking them on shorter walks, as long as they remain active enough in order to stay healthy and fit.

Boerboels are great family dogs, who adore children and can be very protective, something we will look into in more detail later on. They are also normally great with other animals, and while two dogs of the same sex might butt heads more than others, when they are socialized properly, Boerboels will be able to get along with most other pets.

CHAPTER 2

Is a Boerboel Right for Your Lifestyle?

> "Boerboels are best suited in a home with strong owners who can keep consistent expectations and have experience with large guardian breeds. That being said, they are excellent with children as long as the children are supervised and taught to be respectful. They make really good family dogs."
>
> BEVERLY SHUPE
> *Tall Oak's Kennel*

It is important to be prepared when bringing a new pup into your life. Even if you are willing to adapt to the pup's needs, it makes life so much easier when you know what to expect and can plan accordingly.

In this chapter, we will be exploring some of the things that you can generally expect from a Boerboel.

Different sizes

I mentioned the average height and weight of a Boerboel earlier. If the size of your full-grown dog is important to you, then it is important to meet the parents before you commit to a puppy. Viewing the parents could also be important if you are thinking about getting a dog to compete in shows. For many dog competitions, the dog needs to fit into the industry standard for weight, height, and coloring; otherwise, it can't compete.

Most really good breeders can also give you a good indication of how big they think your dog will get. They have experience with puppies and their growth rate. Looking at factors like how big a puppy's paws are might help; in my experience, it does give a good indication. But bigger isn't always better. For example, one of my dogs was massive. Standing on all fours, he could set his head on my chest when I was standing, and I am not all that short. He was super muscled, and he weighed a ton. Or at least it felt like it when you had to get him in the car to take him to a vet or somewhere else. Later he started having major issues with his joints, so exercise became a problem, and then his weight became difficult to control, making the problem even bigger.

Conversely, my female Boerboel was tall and muscled, but she didn't have such big paws or such a large build. Though both her parents were massive, she didn't turn out that way.

If you want a smaller dog, then you should probably consider a different breed altogether or a Boerboel who is crossed with a smaller breed. That said, lineage only goes so far, and dog size can still vary widely.

Photo Courtesy
of Daniela Thompson

Energy levels from puppy to senior dogs

> "Boerboels are fairly adaptable. They have varying levels of energy, dependent upon the individual dog. Room to exercise is important, and apartments are probably not an ideal environment, especially for a young dog. I don't feel a Boerboel is an appropriate dog for a first-time dog owner, as they are quite intelligent and can work diligently to outsmart their people to get their way in all things."
>
> KATE NICHOLSON
> *Wilby Boerboels*

In my experience, it is normally around the two-year mark that a Boerboel pup goes from having a puppy brain to becoming an adult Boerboel. Before that, everyone is the dog's friend. Then he starts to get more protective, and the sometimes-hyperactive energy levels go down.

Adult Boerboels can become pretty lazy if you aren't careful. We had a massive garden where the dogs could play, but they preferred spending most of their time on the back porch and taking a nap.

Their characteristics do lean more toward being couch potatoes, but they are generally up to go with you on a new adventure too. So if you want a large dog that is willing to live more of a laid-back lifestyle with flashes of adventure sprinkled in between, then a Boerboel might just be a perfect fit for your home.

Training

Smart, determined, and incredibly loving, your Boerboel pup wants to make you happy. The breed is smart, so training should be fairly easy. But if you aren't consistent or don't show your new dog that you are sure of what you are teaching him, then he might decide that he knows what is best and do his own thing.

We will go into more detail on training later on in the book, but to decide if a Boerboel is best for you, all you really need to know is that they can be stubborn. They are very smart dogs who understand what is expected of them, but they don't always feel like doing it, so you will need patience and consistency.

Photo Courtesy of Keith Mullins

Shedding and drooling

In theory, Boerboels don't really shed all that much. But because they are so massive, even a little bit of shedding can result in a lot of hair all over the place. Regular brushing can help to lessen the amount of loose hair. I liked brushing my dogs around once a week. Regular bathing can help too.

The same thought applies to drool—Boerboels may not drool a lot, but since they're so big, even a small amount can be, well, large. Leica, one of my dogs, only drooled when she went for car rides. I would have to cover the back seat with extra towels to make sure the entire seat wasn't wet by the time we got to our destination. My niece once decided she wanted to sit with Leica in the back seat on our way to the vet. I did warn her, but I don't think she entirely believed me. When we got to the vet, my niece's arms, shirt, and pants looked like they had been sprayed with water. A big dog can equal lots of drool.

Relationships with family and other pets

> **"**
>
> *"Boerboels thrive in a family environment, bonding very closely to the younger members. They love human contact and are very calm around the home, and despite their size, they are very easy to live with."*
>
> MARK BEASLEY
> *Topguard Kennels*
>
> **"**

When my last Boerboel was around two, I adopted a small parrot. At times, to make sure he got enough fresh air, I would put the parrot outside when it was nice out. If any wild birds came too close, trying to eat the bird food that he dropped, he would freak out. He did this once or twice before my Boerboel realized what the issue was. From then on, she would chase the wild birds away and would also lie down next to the bird's cage, standing guard whenever he was outside. While my dog was next to the cage, the bird would climb down to eye level, and the dog would lick him through the safety of the bars. Her ears were bigger than the bird's entire body, but she was so gentle and soft with this little scared creature.

That story illustrates how Boerboels generally are really gentle, caring dogs that won't hurt your other animals and children on purpose, especially if they grew up with them and were socialized with them properly. But again, size can be a factor. When our big Boerboel leaned against you, it was difficult to stay standing even as an adult. If your dog gets really excited and jumpy with small animals underfoot, it can be disastrous—even tragic. Boerboels can easily injure a smaller animal or even a small child without at all intending to do so. This is key to keep in mind when considering whether or not you should bring one of these gentle giants into your home.

If you want a dog that will fit into your lifestyle and family without requiring a lot of change from your daily habits, then it is wise to carefully consider whether a Boerboel is the dog for you. As noted earlier, they can be high maintenance and very stubborn.

Photo Courtesy
of Conan and Penny Crawford
Bonebluff Boerboels

Legalities

FUN FACT
Origins of the Boerboel

Originating in South Africa, Boerboels were bred primarily for family protection. Echoes of this history can be found in the breed today. Proper and early socialization is critical for this breed and can help your dog avoid developing a fear of strangers or aggression toward dogs of the same sex.

Boerboels aren't exactly little dogs that you can hide in your home, and they attract plenty of attention when you take them out for walks and exercise. Not checking the legalities for your area could cost both you and your dog a lot.

Many places ban these dogs purely for how dangerous they can be if they are trained incorrectly and get aggressive. My Yorkie gets much angrier than any Boerboel I have ever had. When she gets protective when a stranger comes around, I pick her up, and the problem is solved. But when it comes to a dog as large as a Boerboel, they need to be controlled much better. If something does happen and they get aggressive, they can cause serious harm or even death. Many places ban the breed in hopes of reducing the risk. Additionally, Boerboels are also known to be used as fighting dogs, which can give the breed an unfairly bad name.

Housing requirements

These are not apartment dogs. Even if you take a Boerboel pup out for walks regularly, he still needs access to a yard where he can run and play. Some people prefer to keep Boerboels in a fenced-in yard, but you still need to make sure that you spend plenty of time with your dog. They aren't a breed that can be alone all the time.

We had a massive garage connected to our house, and the dogs always came in that way. It was connected to where we worked and watched television, and they could go out into the yard by the same route. They were with us all the time but were still able to go and play when they needed to.

Photo Courtesy
of Desré Jacobs

Cost

Everything is just bigger with a Boerboel. From simple things like giant dog beds to sturdy toys to how much they eat, costs are naturally going to be higher when you buy or adopt a dog this big, and this includes even basic health care. Things like tick and flea treatment either cost more per pill when you buy them for a giant dog, or you need to give a lot more medication per treatment, which also makes it more expensive. Vet treatment can go up by as much as $500 per trip to the vet, just by having a giant breed instead of a regular-sized breed.

Just getting your new puppy could already be expensive. Boerboel puppies can cost anywhere from $2000 to $4000 in America, depending on how valuable a dog's bloodline is, where the dog is, if the breeder is willing to ship the dog, and how in-demand the puppies are. Adopting can be much less pricey. You might not have the same guarantees or the same control when it comes to adoption, but you will still get a dog that loves you just as much.

Start-up costs will be more with a Boerboel, so for the first year, your new puppy can cost you a lot just to get everything set up. Later on in the book, I provide a list of items you'll need to have on hand before your puppy's arrival. If you can't afford to buy everything at once, I would suggest getting a few things over time for a few months before you get your puppy. That way, the start-up costs are broken up over time, and you'll still have everything you need by the time that you bring home your new dog.

Absolutely everything is bigger with a Boerboel than with an average-sized dog. At the same time, Boerboels also have bigger hearts than any other dogs, so the love is supersized too. It is all worth it, in my opinion, but it is important to know what you are getting yourself into.

Control

Even things like taking your Boerboel on a walk can be more challenging than normal due to his size. He needs to be really well trained right from the start. Because if he isn't and he decides to chase something, say a squirrel, then he might be taking you for a walk instead of the other way around.

Case in point: I leash-trained one of my Boerboels inside our fenced yard. He was walking perfectly, not pulling or tugging and really seemed to enjoy it. One day we walked to the gate. There, the dog froze and refused to move any further. I tugged. I pulled. I begged. I tried snacks. He was not budging. I think in his mind, he was not allowed to go outside the gate, and there was just no way that I could convince him otherwise. If we walked

Photo Courtesy of Monica Sciocatti

back inside, he would walk next to me, loving it. But as soon as we got to the property line, he would lie down, and it would be game over.

The point being, of course, that because of a Boerboel's size, being able to control your dog is more important than ever. In the story above, I could have simply picked up a smaller dog, but that isn't something you can do with a Boerboel. If you aren't willing to invest the time in proper training, then a Boerboel might not be the best fit for you.

If you have considered all of these factors very carefully and have determined a Boerboel is right for your lifestyle, then it's time to move on to the best part: finding a pup that is best for you and starting to prepare for bringing it home.

CHAPTER 3

Preparing Your Home and Family

> "
>
> *"This breed needs guidance and a firm hand from day one when brought home at eight weeks of age. They can tend to be bouncy and very playful and need to have their energy directed in a positive way. A new owner should always choose safe chew toys that cannot be torn apart or swallowed. Electrical cords should be placed in conduits; things such as bottle caps and children's toys, such as marbles, jacks, LEGOs and other choking or intestinal blockage hazards, should be kept out of the dog's reach. Things such as watch batteries, as well as other small batteries, should never be within the dog's reach, as swallowed batteries can be fatal. Also, keeping the dog in a fenced area is the safest way to ensure it does not wander off or get out into the road. Boerboels can dig under a fence, so being sure additional fencing is buried a few feet beyond the ground line is a good idea."*
>
> MICHELLE CONVIS
> *Adara Ridge Boerboels*
>
> "

Now that you have chosen your Boerboel, it is time to start getting your home ready for the newest member of the family. Most normal households hold lots of dangers for small children and dogs. As such, there are things to take care of in and around the house that could be safety hazards when you bring your new dog home.

Boerboel puppies can be a bit chewy, but normally if they have enough toys to chew on, then they leave your things alone. So, we will talk about getting the things you need to make the transition into your house as easy as possible.

Photo Courtesy
of Danielle Radey
Mae Boerboels

But first, how can we prepare our home?

Making the inside safe

There are a lot of dangers inside the house that need to be taken care of before bringing your dog home.

ENSURE YOUR DOG CAN'T REACH TOXIC SUBSTANCES.

There are a lot of foods that humans can eat that can be fatal to a dog. Make sure that food, medicine, and household cleaning products are all stored away and/or out of reach.

It might be a good idea to invest in some childproof cupboard locks, especially for cupboards that are floor-level. You would be surprised by what a determined puppy can do if it really wants to get into something.

Later on, we'll go into more detail about the health of dogs and which human foods they can and can't eat.

AVOID TEMPTATION.

Putting things like electric cords or wooden ornaments out of puppy sight might be the best way of ensuring your new baby doesn't get any ideas. You also need to remember that the puppy may already weigh quite a bit, so ensure there is nothing breakable that could be destroyed during playtime when the dog is running around.

Basically, moving everything out of reach that you don't want your puppy to destroy might be a good plan. I like to gradually start putting things back as I start to trust my dogs. I'll discuss that further in the chapter on training.

Areas like bathrooms can be temptations because they have lots of things that can

HELPFUL TIP
Toxic Houseplants for Dogs

Houseplants are beneficial for home air quality, but your leafy décor could be toxic for your pup. Ivy, Pothos, and peace lilies are just a few varieties of plants that are toxic to dogs and cats when ingested. During the puppy phase, it's best to keep any poisonous plants out of reach of your dog. Positive reinforcement training and repellent sprays are other effective methods for teaching your dogs that the houseplants are strictly off-limits! Remember that Boerboels grow quickly and what may be out of reach in the first few months will soon be accessible as your dog grows.

seem like puppy toys to an inquisitive new pup. Just think about things like toilet paper rolls. They are super fun to destroy and tear apart. Teaching puppies that the paper is off limits right away might save you a lot of trouble later on.

In the beginning, it might be easier to just remove the temptation for a little while until your dog is trained. They could reach the toilet paper holder almost from the moment they came home. So temporarily putting it higher might just be easier.

PREPARE YOUR CHILDREN'S ROOMS AND KEEPING THEIR TOYS SAFE.

Children's rooms can be a big temptation too. Making sure that there is nothing around that can be seen as a doggy chew toy is essential to avoiding major conflict. You do not want your new pup to steal a sentimental teddy bear, for example, and tear it to pieces.

I didn't have children, but I did have a dog, Gabby, who had a teddy that she adored. Ever since she was a pup, she walked around with that thing like it was her safety blanket. It was super cute—but then we got a new pup.

Gabby adored the new puppy. When they were eating, the puppy could come and eat right out of our older girl's bowl, and Gabby wouldn't mind. The only thing that was off-limits was Gabby's teddy bear. One day we saw teddy stuffing everywhere. The pup had ripped that thing to shreds. I felt so bad, and Gabby would not play with the puppy for the rest of the day. So consider both your children and other pets when preparing your house for your new Boerboel.

CHECK FOR OTHER HAZARDS.

Again, this is a case of different homes having different dangers. For example, if you have a staircase in your home, it's really important to make sure that the stairs have a baby gate installed.

Loose rugs in your home can be a temptation and a danger at the same time. Playing puppies can slip on loose rugs when running. And they can also start to chew on them. Making sure that they are anchored or taken away for the time being might just be better at first.

Potted plants can be a danger and a temptation at the same time too. Some plants are poisonous to dogs, and puppies don't always have the instinct to stay away from poisonous plants. This might be even more dangerous indoors when a Boerboel pup gets bored. We will speak a bit more in-depth about what types of plants can be hazardous in the next part, but for indoor plants, there are a number of ornamental plants that could be a danger.

Some flowering plants like Amaryllis can be very dangerous if your puppy consumes it at all. Daffodils can cause cardiac and intestinal problems, such as vomiting and diarrhea, and even tremors. Putting potted plants too high to reach might be the answer. Or get covering or netting to place around your plants to protect them from your dog and, in turn, to protect your puppy from the toxins in your potted plants.

Go through your house and look at everything objectively. If you see anything that would be a danger to a human newborn, then chances are that it will be dangerous to a dog. Puppies are still babies; the only difference is that they are a lot more mobile and can get into a lot more trouble immediately.

Preparing the outdoors

Preparing the outside of your house for your new puppy is just as important as preparing the inside, especially if you are going to let your dog spend any amount of time outside unsupervised.

PROTECTION FROM THE ELEMENTS

If you are planning to have your dog spend any time on their own outdoors, then you need to make sure that you prepare an area where they can be safe and comfortable. They need to have a shaded spot to be comfortable in when it is warm.

Making sure that they have a safe and comfortable place in any weather is important. We will talk about the gear you will need in the next section, but preparing the outdoors for your Boerboel's safety and comfort is really important.

Make sure they will have all the fresh cool water and fresh food they could need and a safe space to live in.

TOXIC PLANTS

There could be hidden dangers in your garden that you never realized could be deadly to the new Boerboel that you bring home.

Different palms, for example a sago palm, can be really dangerous because all of the parts of the plant can be highly toxic to a dog, and what makes it even more dangerous is that many dogs find them incredibly tasty—not the best combination. If a dog consumes enough of the plant, it can lead to liver failure and can even kill a puppy.

There can also be hidden dangers in your veggie patch. Tomatoes that are green and the rest of the tomato plant can be a serious hazard to your new pup. They can slow the heart rate and cause general confusion while also creating gastrointestinal problems and drowsiness.

Another plant that humans assume is probably very healthy and completely fine would be the aloe vera plant. But even if it is great for our skin and delicious to drink, it can cause nervous system depression and lethargy, among other things, if a dog chews on it. Oleander, begonia, chrysanthemum,

Photo Courtesy
of Chris Visser

and even tulips are all flowering plants that can be really dangerous for your dog to chew on. Some can even be toxic if your dog only inhales them.

But it is possible to keep your garden intact while still keeping your puppy safe. Things like netting around your dangerous plants can keep them safe until your dog is used to them and over the stage that he will suddenly start chewing on them.

FENCES

While Boerboels aren't big jumpers, a picket fence might not be enough to keep your new family member inside. You don't need an eight-foot-tall fence or one that's dug super deep, but a fence will be necessary.

Making sure that the fence is made from very sturdy material is also pretty crucial. You don't want the entire thing coming down because your large dog leaned against it. Steel palisade is a favorite of mine; it allows the dogs to be able to see the outside world while still keeping them safe.

SWIMMING POOLS

If you have a pool, it is really important to have safeguards in place to make sure that your dog can't accidentally fall in without having any way to get back out.

A small fence around your pool area is always safest for children and pets, but getting a pool cover that is sturdy enough to bear the weight of your dog might be a safe alternative. Make sure that your dog is kept especially safe until you are able to teach him to swim.

OUTBUILDINGS AND GARAGES

Making sure that outbuildings and your garage are puppy safe is vitally important too. You might not think your dog will ever be in there, but you can never be entirely sure.

I once knew a family that kept all of their harmful things outside in the garage on a shelf that should have been too high for the dog to reach. The garage was normally closed, so the dog shouldn't have been in there in the first place. But one day, someone left the garage open just a little bit, and somehow the dog climbed up high enough to reach the rat poison. Since a lot of those poisons taste sweet, he ate quite a bit before his family found him. They took him to the vet, who tried all day and all night, but the dog couldn't be saved.

The same goes for sharp tools or smaller objects like screws that a puppy might be able to swallow. Besides the possibly life-threatening side of things,

Photo Courtesy
of Danielle Hansen

an operation to remove an obstruction in your dog's intestines can cost thousands of dollars.

It is way easier and safer to just make sure that all the areas of your home are safe in the first place.

Preparing your kids for the new dog

In addition to preparing your home for the new arrival, teaching your kids and other pets how to handle the new puppy is super important. Kids need to know what type of behavior is okay with their dog and what really isn't. I have heard people say that if a new dog nips their kids, he will be rehomed straight away. But I always think in terms of any new baby.

If you bring a newborn human home, you won't allow children, whether your own or those belonging to friends, to play with the infant unattended or expect the new baby to be the one in charge. You will look after every interaction and make sure that the children are acting appropriately around the baby. The same can be said for a new puppy.

TEACHING SMALL CHILDREN

Small children are completely able to learn how to have proper care and respect for pets. That said, getting them ready before the new family member comes home is best. Start by showing your kids pictures of the puppy.

Then, you can start to talk about behavior that must be avoided, like pulling ears or tails, sitting on top of the dog, or trying to take away his food or snacks while he is eating. You might ask a friend with a dog to let your kids practice proper dog treatment.

Teach children simple things like how to be gentle and how they can react if the puppy gets too hyper and jumpy. Explain that they will make the puppy sad if they pull his tail or take his toys away to tease him. Layout concrete rules that are clear and easy to follow.

You can also help children be a part of getting ready for the dog by letting them choose a dog toy or a blanket. The entire experience should be really positive because then kids will be excited and look forward to meeting their new friend.

OLDER CHILDREN

Children can for sure be part of teaching the new dog and training him. Just like children, dogs learn best through play, so who better to help teach your Boerboel than his new best friends?

Discuss aspects of pet care that older children will be in charge of. For example, discussing when and how much the new puppy will eat can help children get ready for their new dog-care responsibilities. Depending on their age, you can have your kids help with research on subjects like the best types of dog food or where to take your dog to socialize him once he is fully vaccinated.

29

Older children can also help clean up after a Boerboel and even walk him, among other important chores. When I was a teenager, I was the only one who could bathe my dog. She would refuse to sit long enough or still enough to give anyone else the time to wash and rinse her. But for me, she would patiently wait.

Photo Courtesy
of Maria Tierra

So, there are a lot of ways that older children can be involved with the care of their new dogs. You can also teach them what they should expect from their friends or other children when they come over and what they shouldn't allow when it comes to your new Boerboel.

Teaching children about pet care can teach them a lot of life lessons in general.

Other pets

There are ways to get your other pets ready for your new pup's homecoming. For example, if you have met the dog that will eventually become yours, you could have him lie on a blanket during a visit. Then, you could give that same blanket to your dog so that he could get used to the smell.

Obviously, the initial introductions are going to need to be gradual, making sure that your other pets aren't scared or jealous. The biggest part of getting other pets ready is when you bring the new dog home. You have to ensure that your other pets feel comfortable and that you are giving them all of the attention that they are used to and deserve.

Make sure that your other pets have a safe place where your older pets can go to relax if having a new pup in the house becomes too much for them. For example, older dogs could have a quiet area where they can go to have some quiet time. You could even put up a small fence or an obstruction that your older dog can climb over and your pup can't jump over.

If you have a cat, you might create safe, elevated areas that your cat can jump up onto and where they can relax if having a rambunctious puppy becomes tiring. Giving them a way out might also save the puppy from getting scratched if they keep pushing their luck.

If you have a parrot as I do, then you might be worried about introducing your new pup to your parrot. The dog can easily injure the bird without meaning to. Introducing your dog to your bird takes a lot of care and supervision. When I got my Yorkie, I spoke to my vet about this subject. It might be a much smaller dog, but the same rules apply.

You need to supervise every interaction at the start and make sure that your dog does not become overly excited. The vet said that we want the dogs to become a little bit afraid of the bird. You even want them to nip the dog in warning. But when the dog grows up with your bird, they will start to feel like part of their pack. So, they won't hurt them later on. Even if they chase birds outside, they won't hurt members of their own family.

I would still advise that you should never leave them alone unsupervised when your bird is not in the safety of the cage. I never want to underestimate the power of instinct if the bird suddenly flies or behaves in a manner that triggers the hunting instinct in your pup. And you also want your bird to have his own safe and happy space.

Getting the gear you will need

A puppy needs a lot of gear, especially if this is your first dog. You need to make sure that everything you buy is sturdy and strong. Otherwise, chances are they aren't going to last very long. The size of the pup's jaw means that they will need stronger gear than most other dogs will need.

For some objects like the water and food bowls, you can get the adult size pieces right from the start. For others, like leashes and harnesses, you will need to get the puppy-sized version first and then buy bigger sizes as your dog grows.

FOOD

Getting the best puppy food that you can afford is the most important thing to buy first. We will be going into a bit more detail in the chapter on dog nutrition.

The breeder or your vet might be able to give you the best advice on food. It is pretty important to find out what food your dog was eating before you got him. It might not be what you want to feed him long-term, but to avoid stomach upset, you should only gradually switch your new Boerboel over to your preferred choice of food.

Also, feeding a young pup puppy dog food is a must. It might be tempting to just buy adult dog food right from the start, especially if you already have an older dog. But for the development of strong bones and a healthy adult dog, you need to feed them puppy food that will assist in their growth.

HELPFUL TIP
Breed Restrictions

Despite their friendly disposition, Mastiffs are frequently banned from apartment complexes and some cities altogether. Though Boerboels are a separate breed, their appearance and temperament can be very similar to the Mastiff. If you're a renter, be sure to check with your landlord or leasing agreement before bringing a Boerboel into your life. Certain cities in Michigan, Washington, and Wisconsin ban Mastiffs outright.

FOOD AND WATER BOWLS

It helps to establish a routine when you start to give your puppy food and water from the same bowl from day one. Don't be surprised if you see a happy dance each time you bring out his food bowl. I generally like to get stainless steel bowls that are big enough to work for an adult dog. Then, you don't need to replace them later, and the stainless steel is easy to clean.

Just make sure to keep stainless steel bowls out of the sun, or your pup might not have cool water on a warm summer day. The other option for a water bowl is one with a tank. This makes it easier to ensure that your dog never runs out of water when you aren't looking.

BEDDING AND KENNELS

If you are going to be leaving your dog in your yard during the day, then getting a waterproof and windproof kennel is very important. Your Boerboel needs somewhere comfortable and safe to relax in.

You will need to decide if you are going to crate train your pup, and if you are, then you need to get a crate that is big enough for your dog to be able to stand up and move around in. It should be the dog's happy place. You will also need a bed to place inside the crate. We will discuss training techniques in more detail in chapter 8 of the book.

Getting a dog bed or pillow is also important. It will help with training for the dog to know where he can relax and sleep in peace. Getting beds made from durable fabric, canvas, for example, can help to make the bed last longer even if your Boerboel puppy does succumb to the urge to chew on his new bed.

It can be a challenge to find gear that is big enough to fit your Boerboel. Most pet shops are willing to source extra-large gear even if they don't keep them in stock at all times. Alternatively, online shops like Amazon are a great place to find what you are looking for if you can't find them in the local pet shops around you.

COLLARS AND JACKETS

To get your dog used to walks, you should have leashes and collars ready so that you can start training your Boerboel right from the start. Opinions vary on which types are best, and there are even some legal rules in some areas for bigger dogs. For example, even areas that allow people to keep Boerboels might only allow them if they are walked with shock collars or choking collars. You should be able to find out the rules at the same time as finding out the legalities of keeping a Boerboel in your area.

Personally, I don't like things such as choke collars or anything else that trains through pain. I don't think it is necessary, and I would never be able to hurt any pet. I don't even like a normal collar that could hurt a dog's neck, although this danger is lessened in bigger dogs. I normally have a collar with my dog's name on it that he can wear daily and then a harness and leash for walks. I feel a harness gives you more control over your dog without hurting him, and it is harder to slip out of. Especially in the beginning, when your pup still has a lot of loose skin around his neck, he can slip out of a collar pretty easily.

Boerboels are bred for very warm climates, so if you live in a cold climate that has harsh winters, you might need to get a jacket for your new pup.

GROOMING EQUIPMENT

Trust me, it makes things so much easier if your dog is already used to grooming and getting baths by the time he is older and much bigger. I will discuss grooming in depth in another chapter. For now, know you will need dog shampoo, a dog brush, nail clippers, a dog toothbrush, and dog toothpaste. Having the name of a good groomer might also be a really good idea.

TOYS

Toys, toys, and more toys. Having loads of dog toys that you can rotate is a lifesaver. It helps to fight boredom and chewing. With my Boerboels, I especially like getting a big bag of cow hooves. In my area, they aren't super expensive. Once my dogs have chewed the hooves to bits, I throw them out and give them another one.

They are relatively cheap options to keep your dog entertained. But other great options are the biggest sizes of Kong toys that you can find. They are pretty durable and can last for a while, at least.

Boerboels need extra-large toys; otherwise, you need to be prepared to discard them pretty regularly. Many Boerboels also love balls, but regular tennis balls don't last long, so either get a cheap version that won't hurt your pocket when throwing them away after the first game of fetch. Or get a harder rubber-type ball that won't puncture as easily. But then, if you do go for the rubber version, you will need to take them away between games so that the pup doesn't chew on them and swallow small pieces of rubber when they are left unsupervised.

Getting everything ready before your pup arrives will allow you to spend quality time with him when he arrives without having to run out to find something you might have missed.

CHAPTER 4
Choosing a Puppy

Now that you have decided that you definitely want a Boerboel to come into your family, it is just as important to pick the right dog. Loving this dog unconditionally is going to be a long-term project. So, picking the right puppy is important.

In this section, we will discuss some of the choices that you will have to make when picking your dog and what to consider when making those choices.

Photo Courtesy of Lotte Van Hellemond

Deciding between adopting or buying

This is always the first place to start when considering the dog you want to get. I know many people would just say that adoption is always best, and I do agree that it is incredible if you are willing to do it. But I also believe that there is a place for both adopting and buying.

You have to consider if you are willing to start out with an older dog or prefer a puppy. Chapter 6 of this book will be dedicated to getting you ready if you do start out with an older dog.

Considering things like if you have children or other pets might help you make the decision. There are loads of rewards that come with adoption, but it is true that adopted dogs already have personalities and preferences fully formed when you get them.

If you have a cat, for example, you will need to find a Boerboel that grew up with a cat, and the same goes for other pets. They might have emotional scarring from being mistreated, and you will have to manage those problems. At the same time, there is nothing more rewarding than when an emotionally damaged animal starts to trust you.

Then there is the question of whether or not you can find a Boerboel that is up for adoption in the first place. The breed isn't as available as some other breeds, so it might not even be possible to find one. You might only find a mix, which isn't a bad thing. My one dog was a mix between a Rhodesian Ridgeback and a Boerboel, and she was such a good dog. Note that mix could mean the dog's characteristics might lean toward Boerboel or toward another part of the dog's ancestry.

So, there is a case to make for getting a puppy from a breeder instead of adopting. At the same time, if you want a dog that is a bit quieter and who is over the hyperactive stage, then getting an older dog might be preferable.

If you can't get a dog up for adoption at pounds or shelters,

FUN FACT
How Big Will My Boerboel Get?

Don't let the tiny puppies fool you; Boerboels are considered an extra-large breed. Full-grown adults can weigh from 150 up to 200 pounds and measure around 22-27 inches tall, depending on their sex. Boerboels usually reach their full height between 18 and 24 months but may not reach their full weight until after that time. The first few months of puppyhood can go by quickly, with some Boerboels weighing close to 50 to 60 pounds before six months!

there are other options to consider. Some breeders keep a few dogs from a litter and might be willing to let you have an older dog. Older show dogs or working dogs might also be made available for adoption. Your local Boerboel club or the American Boerboel Association can give you a lead on dogs like that.

Either way, you have to decide what is best for your family and what type of dog will be happiest to come home to you.

Choosing a breeder

"

"Question the breeder extensively. They should have extreme knowledge of the breed in general and of their dogs in particular. They should be able to tell you the good and bad of their dogs and why they paired particular ones together. Also learn about the dogs' parentage—what the parents' temperament, health, energy level, etc., are."

KATE NICHOLSON
Wilby Boerboels

"

None of us want to support puppy mills or make the problem of unethical breeding worse. A puppy mill just keeps animals to breed them as much as possible, without taking the health of the pups or their parents into account. These mills normally have all the dogs in little cages, and the dogs they use for breeding purposes stay in some really terrible conditions. Inbreeding can be a real issue in puppy mills, and the dog you buy from such a place could have serious health issues down the line.

No animal lover would want to support these people who are just using dogs for their own gain and not looking after them at all. That is why choosing a really good breeder is so vitally important. Making sure breeders care for their animals like family and that the mother dog isn't just kept for breeding purposes is vital. Of course, you also want the healthiest, most well-adapted pup you can find too.

That all starts with choosing the right breeder.

ASK A VETERINARIAN

Your local vet can give you some good insights on where to get a happy, healthy Boerboel pup in your area. Since all responsible breeders have their

37

dogs checked by a vet before they go to their forever homes, a vet might have built a relationship with some great breeders in the area that he or she can recommend.

WORD OF MOUTH

This is where it is a great idea to get involved in your local Boerboel club before you even get a dog. If you see a happy, well-adjusted, and well-behaved dog, then you have a really good chance of also getting a great dog from the same family.

BOERBOEL ASSOCIATIONS

Another great place to find reputable breeders is through the Boerboel association that works in your area. The AKC and SABBS can help give you great breeder references and information on past puppies and the families that they went to.

VISIT BREEDERS

Great breeders will be more than happy to give you a tour of their facilities. If they don't want you to visit and would prefer bringing your pup to you, then those are major red flags.

Photo Courtesy
of Janine Bloem
Alessandro Boerboels

Breeders need to allow you to see the puppies' parents, too, so that you can interact with them and see their temperament and how the puppies will look when they are older. If these are deal-breakers for the breeder, then you should probably look elsewhere for your new Boerboel.

Other things to look for when researching breeders include:

NO HIGH-VOLUME DOG SALES

Breeders who have high volumes of puppies going out the door are more likely to be puppy mills. On the other hand, if they have a longer waiting list and only have puppies once or twice a year, then they are more likely to be responsible breeders who are taking the dogs' welfare into account more than the financial profit.

KNOWLEDGE OF THE BREED

A good breeder will have a lot of insight and knowledge of the breed that they are breeding. They will be able to answer the questions that you ask them. So be prepared with some questions, including some you already have the answers to, in order to check each prospective breeder's knowledge on the subject. Asking simple questions like the estimated size that the dog may become can give you a good indication of how knowledgeable the breeder is. Some other possible questions are:

- What is the temperament of a Boerboel?
- What are the housing requirements of Boerboels?
- What types of food do they feed their dogs?
- Where do they keep their dogs? Where do the dogs sleep?
- How do they socialize their dogs?
- What vet do they use?
- What health tests do their dogs receive?

Even when you already have the answers to most of the questions, this kind of interview can help you get to know the breeder and know how much they will be able to assist you after you have received a pup from them. Ideally, they will love the Boerboel breed as much as you do, and they will want to have what is best for the dogs that are leaving their care.

THE BREEDER ASKS YOU QUESTIONS, TOO

Wanting what is best for the puppies means that the breeder will ask you some questions, too. Ideally, a meeting between a breeder and potentially puppy owner is a two-way street where both parties can decide whether or not they are willing to enter into this contract and go into this relationship.

And that is what it should be: a relationship. A relationship where the breeder can request a reference and photos of the pup when he is older, and one where you can contact the breeder if you have any questions later on or just need advice on things like training. Both parties should be comfortable enough with each other so that they don't just complete a transaction and never speak again.

The breeder should ask you questions about how the dog will live and if you are really ready to care for a giant-breed dog. And it is very likely that good breeders will request the first option of buying back the pup if things don't work out and you need to rehome it.

THE PUPPIES ARE SOCIALIZED

Making sure that the pup you get has the right socialization is really important for training purposes later on. Puppies should be willing to come and play with you when you try to interact with them, play with other dogs when you are watching them, and just generally act like happy puppies. If a pup is scared or very timid, this might be an indication that the dogs aren't handled regularly and that the breeder isn't treating the dogs like family pets. It could be an early warning sign to steer clear of that particular breeder.

VACCINATIONS AND AGE

A reputable breeder will also make sure that the dogs have their first vaccinations before they are allowed to go to their forever homes. Good

Photo Courtesy of Angelo Forbes

breeders also won't allow their dogs to be rehomed before they are at least eight weeks old. Some breeders will allow you to take your new puppy at a younger age, but this is bad for the dog in the long run. Puppies need to learn socialization from their mother. Taking them away from their mother earlier is bad for their development and will make your pup harder to train.

Health tests and family history

> "I recommend you first check out the temperament of the puppy to see if it's aggressive at all or scared of real-life situations. Also, check the health history of the parents with the breeder. Boerboels suffer a large number of genetic issues due to the breed's small genetic base in the 1980s."
>
> ERIC PERRY
> *Cavan Creek Boerboel*

A responsible breeder will only breed dogs that don't have a problem with certain genetics that can cause health issues further on in life. They should be able to give you documentation on the health tests they have done, not only on the litter of puppies but on the parents too. If you don't understand all the information, take it to a vet who can interpret it for you and give an expert opinion on whether or not your new pup has the best chance at being a happy, healthy dog for many years.

Hip and elbow reports and scores should be made available for the parent dogs. Female Boerboels should also be tested for vaginal hyperplasia.

These tests won't mean that puppies are guaranteed to be healthy for the rest of their lives, but they will make the chances of having a healthy dog better.

Breeder contracts

Let's look at some things that might be included in a breeder contract.

STERILIZATION

Many breeders will only allow you to buy a puppy if you agree to sterilize the dog as soon as it is old enough to do so. A dog without the stipulation of needing to be spayed or neutered may be more expensive. Remember that show dogs or dogs that compete often can't be sterilized, so know your purpose for buying a puppy before bringing it home.

REHOMING

Many contracts stipulate that if anything happens and you can't rehome your Boerboel to a family of your choice, you are obligated to give the dog back to the breeder. Sometimes the breeder will only ask for the first option of taking the dog back. Other times they require retaking full control of the dog if you ever want to rehome it. This is mostly to discourage people who are serial puppy parents and often rehome adult dogs.

Photo Courtesy of Estie van Zyl

UPDATES

The breeder might also request regular updates and photos of your puppy that they can use as a reference or to post on their website. This can be negotiable.

OTHER CONTRACT STIPULATIONS

Some breeders will have a clause in their contracts where they control things like whether or not you are allowed to show your dog in dog shows. Or they may ask to be allowed to make home visits and to take your dog if they don't feel it is being taken care of properly.

They could also include a clause where you agree to make sure that your dog receives all the vaccinations that the vet deems necessary. Breeders could also ask you to microchip the pup. Some breeders might even microchip the dog before it leaves for its forever home.

Making sure that you are completely on board with all the stipulations of the breeder's contract is essential. Many of the stipulations might be negotiable, so you might want to speak to the breeder with any concerns.

Choosing your puppy

When you are sure that you have chosen the right breeder, then it is time to finally choose your puppy. This can be the fun part, but looking at all those puppy faces can make it really hard to choose. Deciding how feisty or high energy you want your pup to be is important. The breeder knows the pups and can help you pick the right dog for your family. Spending time with the litter of puppies might help you too. You might want to look out for these factors:

- **Is it a very dominant dog?**

This could make it a little bit harder to train the pup, but it could also be a sign of intelligence and an independent puppy.

- **Does the puppy have a potbelly or is it excessively shedding?**

A potbelly can indicate worms, and excessive shedding could also be a really strong indication that the puppy has some underlying health concern.

- **Is the pup shy or timid or really confident?**

Again, this doesn't have to be a deal-breaker; it just depends on the type of puppy that you want to bring into your family. If you want a shy, quiet dog, this might be the puppy for you.

You can also look out for puppies who really like to chew or who seem to be more prone to puppy trouble than the rest of the litter. That could (or could not) mean the puppy will be harder to train. Again, none of this is definitive, but these are all details to consider when choosing your new Boerboel.

After all of those choices, it's time to bring your new puppy home.

Photo Courtesy of Nadine Beattie Beattie Boerboels

CHAPTER 5

Bringing Your Puppy Home

Bringing your puppy home can be really exciting, but it can also be a difficult time. You need to adapt and make sure that the change is as easy for your puppy as possible. Managing the first few days well will set the foundation for your relationship with your new puppy.

Photo Courtesy of Melanie Esparza Santacruz

Bringing your puppy home

> "Try to keep your puppy off of any slippery floors, such as laminated floorboards and smooth tiles. Too much time kept on surfaces with no grip can lead to joint problems. Try to keep your dog on surfaces with a good level of grip, like carpet or rough stone floors."
>
> MARK BEASLEY
> *Topguard Kennels*

At last, the time has come to go and get your pup. It can be a really exciting time. Some breeders give you a puppy pack with some things to take home. This normally includes a small package of the food that the puppy is used to eating, and maybe even a toy or a blanket the dog is familiar with. The food is important because you will need to gradually change the pup's food to what you want him to eat at your home. If you change the food over immediately, then you will probably end up with a dog with an upset stomach.

Taking your dog home is safest by using a crate in the car that has been properly secured. Just having a passenger hold the dog could be dangerous if you get into an accident or have to stop suddenly. But a crate is a safe space where the puppy can relax.

If you are traveling far, then you need to make sure that you give the puppy water and make stops so he can stretch his legs and potty. Remember that the crate needs to be big enough for the dog to stand up and turn around in. He must never be uncomfortable.

When you get home, you need to give the pup time to explore while still keeping a close eye on him. We will deal with socializing him with your other animals shortly, but try to keep everyone as relaxed and happy as possible.

First-night expectations

The adjustment to a new home can be hard for your puppy, and it is up to you to make him as comfortable as possible. You also need to control your expectations on the first night.

The puppy probably won't come when you call right away, and he will almost certainly not be potty trained. I would suggest letting the major

Photo Courtesy of Christopher Mcelhinny

training wait for the first day or two until he is settled in. Obviously, you will take the dog outside to potty, and you won't allow him to do things that you don't want him to do in the long run.

But the first few days are for bonding, not for discipline. Cuddling with your pup, teaching him his name, and just generally loving him is the best way to go for the first few days, in my opinion. Your new puppy is going to be frightened enough without having a strange person speaking to him in a stern voice. Just be kind.

Expect to have to deal with a crying puppy the first night. Before now, he will have slept next to his brothers and sisters and his mother. The best place to let him sleep for the first night is in a contained area inside where you can keep an eye on him. A crate works well for this. We will speak more about crate training in chapter 8, but for now, know that using a crate is great for making sure that a pup doesn't wander off in the night or put himself in any sort of danger when you aren't supervising. In my experience, giving your pup a source of heat, like a hot water bottle that is closed very tightly, can help him feel less alone the first few nights.

If there's a blanket the puppy came with, putting that inside his sleeping area could be helpful too. Otherwise, you can put something of your own, like a shirt or a jersey with your smell on it, with your puppy for comfort. It can help him to settle in and hopefully sleep right through the night.

If he does cry at night, heating up the water bottle and consoling him should help the puppy settle back in and calm down. But please be patient; your new baby will soon be used to his new surroundings and be completely at ease.

It is possible that a pup could sleep right through the night. But for the first few nights, it might be safer to take him out at least once in the middle of the night in addition to right before bedtime and early in the morning. A very young pup might need to go out more than once a night, but generally, after a few days, once will do the trick.

At this stage, a Boerboel pup will probably be eating around twice a day, and you can start transitioning to a new food after a few days of giving him time to settle in and relax in his new environment. You don't want to make too many changes too quickly because stress can give a puppy a runny tummy.

> "
>
> *"Most puppies will need reassurance when going into a new home. Putting the puppy in a plastic tote next to your bed, where you can dangle your arm in at night to pet the pup, tends to help the dog feel less lonely and also begins the bonding process between pup and new owner."*
>
> MICHELLE CONVIS
> *Adara Ridge Boerboels*
>
> "

Choosing a vet

If you have asked a vet for advice on finding your new puppy, then you might already have a good idea of where you want to take your new dog. But otherwise, you might need to find the perfect vet for you and your new fur-child.

Don't be afraid to ask questions. You need to feel completely at ease with the person who is going to take care of your dog if anything ever happens. This is all about preparation. Hopefully, you will only ever need a vet to give your Boerboel his yearly vaccinations and checks. But if anything happens, then you need to have a good relationship with your vet. If your pup also visits the same vet from a young age, he might be more at ease if he ever does need treatment.

Ask questions. For example, if your dog does need hospitalization, how often will you be able to visit him? I had a young Boerboel that very suddenly got sick. We took her to a vet, and they did every test that they could think of, but they couldn't figure out what was wrong with her. They eventually concluded that it was a blood infection. The worst part was that I was only allowed to see her once the entire time she was in the hospital. They had

Photo Courtesy of Alex and Phyllis Patterson

a visitation policy that you were only allowed to see your dog every second day, and on one of those days, they were treating a wild cat from a sanctuary, so I wasn't allowed to visit. It felt like I had abandoned her.

By the time she slipped into a coma, I hadn't seen her for days, and I never got to say goodbye. It is still one of my biggest pet parent regrets. Since then, one of my first questions to a new vet has always been what the clinic's policies are when it comes to dogs that are in hospital.

Something else that might be worth considering with a Boerboel is a mobile vet who can come to you. With a dog that is as big as a Boerboel, it might be completely worth the slightly higher cost in exchange for the convenience of not having to transport your dog. Even if your dog is trained to get into a car or truck, he might not be able to do so if he is really sick, and lifting such a big dog might be a bit much to handle.

In areas where Boerboels aren't common, it might be really good to research vets that already have experience with the breed or who at least know how to handle giant breed dogs if there aren't any veterinarians with Boerboel experience in your area.

The hours that they work could also be a factor when choosing your vet. There is nothing worse than having a sick pup over the weekend and having to wait until Monday to be able to get them help. A vet who has weekend hours is much better when an emergency strikes. Some, like the one I have now, even have 24-hour, 7 days a week emergency lines if your dog does have a problem at strange times.

And then lastly, you should probably look at the distance from your home too. If you have a dog that has hurt itself or gotten sick, then you don't want to have to drive for an hour in order to get them seen.

Getting your dog comfortable with the vet

This is really important to do since it will make going to the vet much easier for both you and your dog. Here are some tips to get your dog comfortable with going to the vet.

- When your dog is really young, take him to the vet often. Getting him checked out and weighed is not only a great way to make sure that your dog is healthy, but it is also a great way for him to get used to vet visits. The vet can also help you with clipping the dog's nails if you are scared to do so yourself.

- Play with your dog or go for a walk with him before you leave for the vet. If he is tired and relaxed, he won't be as nervous.

- When your Boerboel is young, keep him on your lap so that he doesn't get over-excited by the other animals in the waiting area. Also, keep him on leash. That way, it will be part of the routine when he is grown. It should be said that many vets prefer having a large breed dog like a Boerboel wait in the car until it's the dog's turn to be seen, but normally that is only when they are fully grown.

- While you are waiting in the waiting room, be calm yourself, and that will transfer to your dog. Speak to him softly and in soothing tones. Keep him relaxed.

- Hold your dog when he is young, especially when he is getting vaccines, or hold your hand on him if the vet prefers him standing on the exam table as a puppy. As a grown dog, your Boerboel will probably be examined on the floor. But giving that assurance that you are still there can help to soothe the nerves of a nervous puppy.

- Give your dog a treat after the vet visit to end the experience on a positive note.

Socializing with other pets

Earlier, we discussed getting your older pets ready for the new arrival. They need a safe space to go to if they want to get away from the new puppy.

For cats and older dogs, having some sort of clear barrier between them at first might be the least stressful option. Cats might take a bit more time to get used to the new addition, so you might need to keep them separated for longer than with other dogs. Look at the situation and decide when both animals are at ease and when it is a good time to allow a little bit more contact.

Other dogs might be friendly faster, but you will still need to monitor the situation before allowing them to be on their own and unsupervised. At first, I like to hold a pup and bring it down to my older dog's height while still holding on. Then you can look out for any worrying behavior from the older dog. Let the dogs smell each other, and gradually, if things seem to be going well, put the pup down. But stick around. If the older dog becomes aggressive or the pup seems overwhelmed, it might be best to separate them again and allow them to gradually get used to each other.

Make sure that your older pets still feel loved and secure in their own position in the family. A puppy takes a lot of work that makes it easy to forget to give your existing pets all the attention they are used to and deserve. Consciously taking time to spend with them helps avoid jealousy and lessens tension or aggression.

If your Boerboel is your first pet, you will still need to make an effort to ensure he is properly socialized with other dogs after he has received all his vaccines. Puppy school, dog parks, and playdates with friends' pets are great ways of getting your dog used to other animals.

If your pup sees a strange animal on a walk, it will be easier to control him if it is something he is used to already. Socializing ahead of time is much easier than trying to slow down a massive pup who wants to chase a cat because it is the first time he has seen one.

Photo Courtesy of Karen Kloppers

Bonding

Bonding with a new pup is one of the most fun and rewarding parts of getting your new baby. There is nothing quite like that first time that your pup comes when you call his name. But it takes some effort to bond with your new baby and to get to know him.

FEEDING TIME

Studies have shown that a dog will bond the fastest with the person feeding him the first few months in a new home. So, if you want your puppy to specifically bond with your kids, then it might be a really great idea to allow the children to feed the dog. Or, if you want the dog to bond with everyone equally, then it might be best for everyone to take turns feeding him.

PLAYTIME

Giant Boerboel babies need to play a lot, and playing with them is a great way of bonding and even starting to train them. Playing fetch, starting to teach the dog tricks, playing tug-of-war, or just running around in your backyard can all be great ways of bonding with your new baby. Just remember that a Boerboel baby still needs a lot of rest and naps.

CUDDLING

Boerboel pups can be a bit nippy at the start. The best time to cuddle with your puppy is after all his energy has been spent, and he just wants to sleep. Even in households where your Boerboel won't be allowed inside, lying on a blanket on the grass could be a great way to bond with your new baby. It also helps to teach him that quiet time can be just as rewarding as playtime.

WALKS

Another opportunity to bond with your pup is by taking him on walks. He will need to learn how to walk without tugging and pulling, but this will come with time. Initially, just allow the dog the space to get used to going on walks. Allowing him to smell everything and to have fun on walks will make him easier to train in the long run. Just letting him get used to the smells and sounds while out walking and giving him a chance to practice walking on a harness or a leash is the first step of training.

SNACKS, AND TEACHING YOUR DOG HIS NAME

Teaching your Boerboel his new name is one of the most important first steps with your baby. It can also be really fun and a great bonding experience. Calling your dog by his name and giving him a snack each time he comes is a great way to very quickly teach him to respond. Just don't overfeed him. Small training snacks are a great way to teach without creating nutritional issues.

Making your pup feel safe

"

"Make sure your Boerboel has a quiet place with his bed and toys. A crate is a must for a pup to keep him safe and out of things he could get into and which could cause injury to him. It is a good idea to ask the breeder to rub a blanket on littermates or the puppies' dam, so it has the scent on it. You can place the blanket in the crate for the pup to sleep with, helping it feel safe."

BEVERLY SHUPE
Tall Oak's Kennel

"

By this time, you might have had your new Boerboel for a week or so. He will be starting to bond with you. A happy dog is a dog that feels safe with his owner. He is already starting to learn who you are and that you would never hurt or abandon him.

Being consistent with praise and with rules is another way to build a routine that will help your dog feel safe. Routine helps a lot. Feeding your dog at the same time, playing with him, and going on walks can all help to build love and trust and make your new dog feel really happy and safe in his new environment.

HELPFUL TIP
Crate From the Start

Boerboel puppies grow at super speed, with some dogs reaching nearly 60 pounds in four to six months. If you choose to crate train your dog from the start, you may want to err on the side of purchasing a larger crate than you initially need. Many dog crates come with a moveable divider to ensure that your crate size matches your dog size as he grows. However, using too large a crate could result in slower house-training. A good rule of thumb is to make your crate two to four inches longer than your dog, measured from nose to tail.

CHAPTER 6

What if You Start with an Older Boerboel?

Getting an older dog can pose some challenges, as he will already be set in his ways. These challenges are by no means a reason to shy away from adopting an older Boerboel, but being prepared is half of the battle. Let's look at some of the challenges you could face and what you can do to overcome them.

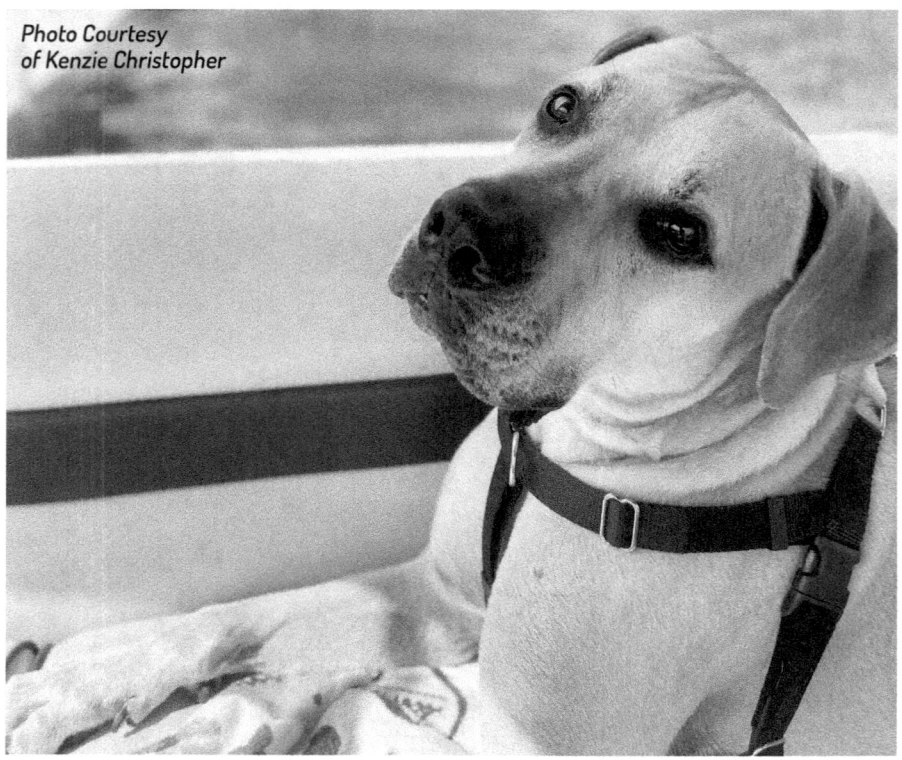

Photo Courtesy of Kenzie Christopher

Patience

This is probably the biggest key when getting an older Boerboel. Have patience. When getting a dog from a shelter, there are no guarantees that you know the full story of what exactly happened before he came to your home. Maybe a loving family gave him up for a good reason, but that in itself is already a massive trauma. Just imagine having people that you adore and who you believe will always love you, drop you off and never come back to get you.

Earning an older dog's trust is rewarding—just don't think it will happen overnight. We have all seen those videos where a dog completely changes right after he gets home and out of the shelter. Some dogs can do that, but most of the time, that is just not the case.

An adopted older dog will be scared. He might flinch when you call; it might be frustrating at times because you have shown nothing but kindness, and the dog is still afraid.

Teaching an older dog basic manners and rules can be a little bit harder, especially if it is a dog that is frightened, and you need to be very careful not to build onto the trauma he has already faced.

If you just stay consistent and patient, it will all be more than worth it in the end. Because these dogs already know the hard and heartbreaking side of life, they appreciate the love that you are giving them so much more.

Children and other pets

It is even more crucial that you make sure to prepare your children and other pets for the arrival of an older dog. A dog that is scared could be dangerous. You don't know what could be a trigger. We had one dog that would get really angry when you touched his back legs or bum area. It turned out the people he was with before would angrily grab him on the behind to drag him away. After some time spent carefully

HELPFUL TIP
Giant Paws Boerboel Rescue

Giant Paws Boerboel Rescue is a foster-based nonprofit dedicated to rescuing and rehoming Boerboels. This rescue provides initial veterinary care and training to homeless Boerboels while they look for their forever homes. To become a foster dog parent or view adoptable dogs, visit www.giantpawsboerboelrescue.org.

Photo Courtesy of Katie Brown

touching him and giving him warning when doing it, our dog learned that we weren't going to hurt him, and he relaxed.

But it was up to us to learn what his triggers were first. Everything that an older dog does is something he has learned to protect himself, some-times in terrible conditions. You have to reteach him, and this takes not only patience but a bit of extra care when it comes to the safety of children and other animals.

The shelter can normally tell you how the dog that you are looking to adopt reacts with other dogs and cats, and you should take this into consideration before making your final decision. If you have another dog, it might also be best to bring it for a visit with a prospective sibling while the Boerboel is still at the shelter.

The last thing you want to do is adopt a dog from the shelter and then be forced to take him back for the safety of your other pets. Being absolutely sure of the decision is the safest and fairest thing to do for yourself and the dog.

OLDER CHILDREN

Children of all ages can be involved when choosing your Boerboel from the shelter, and they can visit with the dog, too, before the final decision is made.

Getting older children to do some of the bonding activities with the dog might be a really great way to put him at ease. Children might not be as intimidating as an adult. Just know that a dog might become really overprotective of kids, even "guarding" them from you, his parents. Boerboels have a really strong protective instinct, and a dog that has been hurt before will be even more protective when he finally finds a family.

SMALLER CHILDREN

Teaching young children to be really gentle is vital. Let them play with the dog, making sure that they never tease him. Letting kids give the dog treats is a great bonding tactic. If you aren't sure how nicely the dog will take the treat, the child can put it down in front of the dog at first.

So, supervising any interactions between your Boerboel and children is crucial in the first few weeks and months until you know your dog won't hurt your child or vice versa.

Past trauma

Just like with humans, past trauma can change a dog's personality. And it can be harder when you don't know the extent of the trauma that a dog has faced.

You are going to be in charge of figuring out the ways that you need to make up for the past trauma that your pup has faced in order to make

Photo Courtesy
of Julie Domelow

sure that he understands that he is now safe. Once you get over that hurdle, it should start getting easier to bond with your new dog. But be aware, post-traumatic stress disorder is a real thing that happens to animals too. That means that a dog can seem completely fine, but then something can trigger that stress, and the dog can be traumatized all over again.

Expectations

Limiting your expectations will help so that you don't get frustrated if the bond with your adopted older Boerboel takes longer to build than you anticipated. But at the same time, it is important to celebrate the milestones along the way, such as the first time a dog comes to you when called.

There are also older dogs available that have no trauma and that are just looking for forever homes. If that is what you want, you might just need to be willing to travel a little further to get the perfect dog.

The bonuses of getting an older dog

Getting an older dog is not only rewarding, but it can be much easier than getting a puppy. An older dog won't be as hyperactive as a young pup. A dog that has lived with a family should be trained pretty well. It also may already be used to interacting with kids and other animals.

Photo Courtesy of Angelo Forbes

CHAPTER 7

Behavior to Check from the Start

Every puppy has some challenges and behavior that you need to check from the moment that you take him home. But when a pup gets as big as a Boerboel gets, the time that you have to correct such behavior is shorter. They grow rapidly, and the damage they can cause with bad behavior grows pretty quickly too. That is why you should start correcting your pup as soon as the two of you are bonded. Correcting bad behavior doesn't mean that you are nasty with your dog or that you ever hit him or punish him. Correction combined with a stern voice and a reward normally do the trick pretty quickly.

Jumping

When your pup is going to eventually outweigh some humans, it is crucial that you make sure that he doesn't jump on people.

When I was really young, I helped out with some office work for a guy who had a really sweet but badly trained Boerboel. I had a small car, and she would jump up against it. There were actually scratches on top of my car as she got so excited when I stopped by. Really not the best thing when you have people visiting.

You also probably don't want your dog jumping on an elderly relative or any unsuspecting friend. Boerboels are heavy enough to hurt someone just by being overly friendly. The best time to correct this is when your dog is small.

When a puppy gets really jumpy because he wants attention, don't give him attention. Tell him to sit without touching him. Or when he doesn't know how to sit yet, show him what you want by giving him some soft pressure on the bum area. Then give him pats and treats as a reward for sitting.

Do this each and every time the dog starts to jump, and he will quickly learn that if he wants attention, he needs to sit and wait for you to give it. Get your friends to do the same when they come over to visit.

*Photo Courtesy
of De Ron Arneaud*

Biting/Teething

A nippy puppy is kind of part of the deal, especially when he is teething and his gums are itching. But when your dog's mouth becomes bigger than both your fists combined, then you really don't want him thinking that nipping you is okay.

Even when they are small, little pup teeth can be razor-sharp, and they can cause some serious pain if you allow a dog to nip. You can teach your dog how to stop. When he starts to chew on your hand, make it into a fist and firmly say "no." Then, if the dog stops, give him something that he is allowed to chew on, like one of his toys. Stop playing with him when he bites you. Then when he chews on his toys instead of you, you can play with him again. Also, teach your dog which things he is allowed to chew on to help him to know what things are off-limits.

Photo Courtesy of Hilary Calton

Food aggression

In my experience, Boerboel puppies don't have a lot of food aggression, so it is really a matter of making sure that they don't develop it.

Don't allow children to tease pets by taking away their food. Then a dog is more likely to try to resource guard because he is worried.

An older dog that is scared of losing his food is probably a dog that knows what it is to be starving. His behavior will probably start to get better as he gets used to always having enough food.

What helped with my dogs that had food trauma was to make sure there was always a little bit of food available to eat at any time. For the first few days, a dog might keep eating it all, but eventually, he learned that he would always have food, and he didn't need to fight to survive anymore.

HELPFUL TIP
Down, Fido

Big dogs who jump in greeting can be a nuisance, especially if you have children in your home. A 200-pound Boerboel could easily knock someone over in his enthusiasm for kisses. Dogs most likely jump out of excitement, so it's a great idea to practice your greeting over and over until your dog is more comfortable with the process. One of the simplest ways to stop your dog from jumping is to withhold attention for this behavior until your dog stops jumping and then offer a treat or reward such as petting. A trainer is always an excellent resource for teaching you how to fix problematic behavior.

Digging

Another thing that you might want to nip in the bud is digging in the garden. Digging is a natural habit, but the problem is that giant dogs equal giant holes. So, if you care what your garden looks like at all, you might want to reach a compromise and allow your dog only to dig in a certain area. If that becomes his favorite spot, then generally, he will leave the other parts of your garden in peace. Putting safety nets around a certain part of your garden could help too.

There are products available to discourage dogs from digging in certain spots, but in my experience, none of them really work. The only thing that does make a difference is consistency, being stern, and filling up the holes that have been dug.

Photo Courtesy of Tina and Ken Burgio

Bottom line: The best thing to stop your dog from forming a digging habit in the first place is to make sure that he isn't bored. Take him on long walks or two shorter ones. Play with him at home, and ensure that he has plenty of toys to keep him entertained when you are at work. Something like a treat dispenser toy is enjoyable to dogs.

Excessive barking

Boerboels aren't excessive barkers. They generally would rather growl at a danger than bark at it. But there are always exceptions to every rule.

But how can you teach a dog to stop doing what he is naturally supposed to do? Being vocal when greeting you or asking for something is completely normal dog behavior. But your neighbors will thank you for teaching your dog not to bark constantly, and it will also help you to know that when your dog is barking, there is really a problem or someone who is around that shouldn't be.

Never shout at your dog for barking. He'll just think it's great that his parents are joining in on the barking fun.

Distraction is the best training technique when it comes to excessive barking. Getting a snack and saying "quiet" in a quiet voice while showing the dog the snack will get his attention better than yelling.

When your dog quiets down, give him the treat. You can also ask him to come into the house and praise and reward him when he obeys that demand. Eventually, you won't need the treat anymore, and you will be able to quiet the dog with just your normal tone of voice.

Photo Courtesy of Wayne and Rebecca Riley

How routines help

Dogs are like children in that when they know what you expect, they are better able to follow through than if they have to guess at what you want from them.

Most aggressive or bad behavior comes from not knowing what to do and also from fear. Routines help with everything. If your dog has food aggression, then having a routine of feeding him at a certain time of day can help him to know at what exact time he'll get food, which will help with his anxiety.

CHAPTER 8
Potty Training

> "Beginning the potty training process from the moment the pup arrives home is important. Start using the same key words, taking him out the same door, and going out to potty approximately at the same time daily. This helps form a routine. Routine is key in properly training your new puppy."
>
> MICHELLE CONVIS
> *Adara Ridge Boerboels*

It can be a lot of work to make sure that your dog is properly potty trained. Of course, if you are planning on having your dog stay outside most of the time, the potty training will start to come easier to him because he will be used to spending most of his time outside, where he's expected to potty. But then you still need to teach him where you expect him to go so that his bathroom is contained to one area, such as one corner of grass. When you consider that a giant dog has pretty giant poops, too, you don't want that all over your yard.

Let's look at some ways that can help you to make sure that your dog's potty training journey is as easy as possible.

Having achievable goals

This is probably the most crucial element in the potty-training journey. Becoming frustrated and fighting with a dog when he makes mistakes is not going to help anyone; the only thing you might achieve is a dog that is scared of you when he needs to do his business and, therefore, ends up hiding it, whether that is outside or in a corner of your bedroom. Or he can become so anxious that he starts eating his own feces. Getting stressed out about the situation is not going to help anyone.

Being consistent

Consistency is key when it comes to getting your dog trained properly. Make sure that you use the same command each time.

Lots of praise

Giving loads of praise is the best way of teaching your dog what you need from him. Praise him each time he goes where you want him to go, and be really over the top with your praise to get your dog excited about doing what you asked of him.

Photo Courtesy of Nadine Beattie Beattie Boerboels

Techniques to potty train

Using the following techniques can help your dog get fast and easy potty-training results.

PHYSICALLY PLACE YOUR DOG WHERE HE SHOULD GO

In the beginning, actually physically picking your dog up and carrying him to the spot where you want him to go might be best. This only applies when you have a puppy, of course. But leading an adult dog consistently to the same place is also vital. You are teaching him to go in one particular spot.

TAKE YOUR DOG OUT AFTER HE EATS OR DRINKS

Taking your dog outside shortly after he has eaten or had something to drink will ensure he is in the right spot when nature calls, making it easier for him to catch on to what you want him to do.

Photo Courtesy of Wendy Lehr

*Photo Courtesy
of Lotte Van Hellemond*

TAKE YOUR DOG OUT AFTER NAPS

Puppies will probably need to go outside almost as soon as they wake up.

TAKE HIM OUT OFTEN

Take your dog out at least every hour or two when he is very young. Puppies can get so wrapped up in playing that they forget and then can't run to their designated potty spot in time.

TAKE YOUR DOG OUT BEFORE BEDTIME AND AFTER WAKING UP IN THE MORNING

Take your dog out just before bedtime and as soon as he wakes up in the morning. Most Boerboel puppies will sleep through the night almost right away. By taking him out before bedtime and as soon as you hear him stir in the morning, you'll set up that all-important routine.

70

HELPFUL TIP
Routine, Routine, Routine

Whether you're house-training your Boerboel puppy or an older rescue pup, routine is an integral part of the process. Boerboels are incredibly intelligent dogs, so learning a routine should be a breeze. Establishing a feeding routine, as well as a potty break routine, will go a long way toward helping your dog learn appropriate elimination etiquette.

This might all sound overwhelming, but it won't be long before you could just open the door for him, and he can go outside exactly where you want him to go, all on his own. And in my experience, this is the quickest way to allow that to happen.

USE A COMMAND

Telling your Boerboel exactly what you want him to do, such as "go potty," helps your dog learn faster. Then, when you need him to go at unusual times of the day, he will still obey the command. For example, if you are going on a road trip and you need him to potty before you go, having an established command can be extremely helpful. If he doesn't go right away, give the command again until he does as you ask. Then give him praise and repeat again the next time it is time for a potty break.

GIVE YOUR DOG TIME

This could be difficult when you are busy with work or something else, but you have to allow your dog the time to remember why he is outside. Puppies are naturally curious, and your Boerboel might get distracted. But then, as soon as you take him back inside, he might remember what he wanted to do and have an accident. By just giving him those extra few minutes to focus, you can help avoid that from happening.

CRATE TRAINING

I have never crate trained a dog, but it does seem to really work. By putting a dog in his crate overnight, you limit the chances that he will wander off and make a mess in your home. Dogs naturally don't want to mess up the inside of their comfortable space, so they will usually try very hard not to have an accident inside the crate at night.

Crate training is also a really good way of sleep training your pup. Just remember that the crate must never be a place where he is sent as a form of punishment or when you are tired of dealing with him. Rather, it should be a relaxing place for him to hang out in—his happy place.

Make sure that the crate you are training your pup in is big enough for him to be able to stand up and move around in. It should have space for a few toys but not be so big that it becomes scary for the pup or be so big that he can do his business in a corner without being inconvenienced. Normally you need a smaller size for when they are a young puppy, and then when your Boerboel gets older, you will need a big crate.

A good rule to remember is to allow them to go in there when they just want to relax during the day too. Leave the door open for them to go in and out. Maybe allow them to eat a snack in there and take naps. Then when you close them up at night, they won't be distraught. Rather they will be going into an area where they enjoy being and know that it is time for quiet time.

LEASH TRAINING

The theory is that when you leash your dog for the first few weeks and keep his leash attached to you, you can monitor him that much more closely. That means keeping him on a leash the entire time he is inside the house.

A long leash still allows the pup to play but keeps him from wandering too far away from you. Some people say this can help a dog potty train within weeks because you are monitoring him so closely you will never miss the moment when he needs to go outside, and you can, therefore, be consistent 100 percent of the time.

How older dogs factor in

If you have an older dog, then you might just have a secret weapon. Older dogs are incredibly useful when it comes to training puppies. Your older pup might just take over training almost completely, and that isn't even limited to potty training. An older dog can demonstrate the behavior that a puppy needs to follow, helping him pick the right spot in the garden and teaching him that going potty inside the house is a mistake.

Older dogs will even teach a younger dog when it is appropriate to bark or how to behave around the family. If this is your first dog, and you put in all of that effort, then it might be something to think about when your dog is older to get him a pup to train and make life easier for you on the next puppy.

However you decide to potty train your dog, do it with a lot of love and care, using a lot of praise and staying completely consistent.

CHAPTER 9
Socializing

> "Do not take your puppy out in public or bring other animals into your home until all puppy shots are complete around 20 weeks of age. This is important, as all pups are susceptible to deadly diseases until all the vaccines in the series of puppy shots are completed. After that time, you can take the puppy for walks on public sidewalks. When greeting other animals, reassure your puppy by talking in a calm voice. You may pet the other animal in the presence of your dog in order for your puppy to see the other animal is okay and of no threat. You may allow others to pet your puppy, but do not allow your puppy to jump up on people or act in an inappropriate manner. Having your puppy fairly well versed in basic obedience will help with this process. Once he is fully vaccinated, you may enroll your puppy in training classes as this is a great way to socialize him on a larger scale with multiple dogs."
>
> MICHELLE CONVIS
> *Adara Ridge Boerboels*

The best time to socialize a dog well is when he is young. That is not to say that older dogs can't learn to socialize, but the challenges and dangers are much greater when a dog is not only older but set in his ways.

In this chapter, we will discuss the importance of a well-socialized dog, how Boerboels deal with children and other animals, challenges, and some techniques that can help you get your dog socialized.

Why is socializing so important?

Dogs that aren't used to other people and animals can be unpredictable and dangerous. And when they are Boerboel-sized, then that problem is going to be heightened tenfold. If you have a dog that can't adapt to other people or animals, and something happens to you, then a lack of socialization very well may be a death sentence for your dog. No one wants that for their beloved pet.

Photo Courtesy of Hilary Calton

When you have a dog that is well socialized, you can bring anyone home, and they can have an easy interaction with your dog. When your Boerboel is not trained well, then the opposite will be true. You will end up having to lock your dog away each time someone comes to visit. By not seeing people regularly, the problem will compound so that the dog becomes even less social. On the other hand, when your pup is trained properly, he will be able to greet any visitor appropriately and then be calm while you visit with your guests, regardless of the dog's large size.

When I see an unfamiliar Boerboel's body language is relaxed and he is socialized well, I have no issue playing with and patting that dog. I know he isn't the type to suddenly turn, so I am just not scared of him. There are smaller dogs that would suddenly do much more damage in my experience. But when people only see a Boerboel's massive size and huge jaws, then that is the only thing they judge the dogs on, so socializing them is even more important because of the intimidation factor.

Socializing from a young age is important because it also helps you build trust with your dog. If you know your Boerboel and are aware of how he is going to react in each situation, you will also go into it much more relaxed and at ease. And dogs pick up on that. For example, if you are walking your dog and another small dog crosses your path, you might become tense if you aren't sure what your Boerboel will do. Then your dog will sense your tension, look at this new intruder, and think that it is the reason you are tense. That will, in turn, make your Boerboel nervous, which could result in problems.

I have heard people say that they don't want to socialize their dogs too much because a friendly dog could be useless as a guard dog. That is a big myth. It does not matter how friendly your dog seems or how happy he is. If you are in danger, he is going to protect you.

Dogs also pick up on social cues. The house where we had many of our Boerboels had a side gate where you could access the backyard. We kept our dogs contained in the back because it was safer for them; there was a problem with people poisoning big dogs. And besides that, we had a massive back garden.

Our dogs loved visitors, but we soon noticed a strange pattern. When our friends came in through the back door, the dogs were happy and excited to see them. When those same friends tried to enter through the garden gate, the dogs would not allow them to enter. Even my own uncle, who would come to take care of the dogs when we were away, would have to call us many times to take the Boerboels away if he needed to bring something in through the side. As you can see, just because a dog is socialized well does not mean he won't be protective.

*Photo Courtesy
of Jason & Tamara McCartney*

Walking your Boerboel pup

A great way to socialize your new dog is to walk him as soon as possible after he comes home and after he's received all his vaccines. Allowing him to interact with other people and other dogs that you come into contact with on your walks will allow him to soon get used to others. Obviously, ask first before getting too close to other dogs or humans. But teaching your Boerboel that other people and dogs are friends while he is still young will help both of you when you get older. It could allow you to go to dog parks, and you might even be able to teach him to go off leash in areas where it is allowed.

You have a big dog. You won't be able to physically stop him if he gets out of control, so his training must be to a standard where he will listen when you tell him to stop. This is as much for the safety of other people and dogs as it is for your own pup's safety.

I can almost guarantee that you will, at some stage during your walks, come upon a dog that is not well socialized and trained. And there is a very good chance that it will be a much smaller dog than your Boerboel. If your dog isn't trained properly either, then the two canines could do some really serious damage if they are challenged. It is at times like this that training really becomes important. You might not fear for your dog's immediate safety, but if two dogs get into a fight, it will almost surely be the bigger dog and its owner who will be blamed for any damage.

Photo Courtesy
of Janine Bloem
Alessandro Boerboels

*Photo Courtesy
of Anna Linkman*

Boerboels and children

I have not had one Boerboel who did not adore children and who was not super protective of them. But, of course, my dogs were socialized with children when they were young pups. You need to supervise children with dogs at a very young age to make sure that neither hurt each other. But giving them this bond from a young age will ensure that no tragic accidents happen later on in life.

Like I said, our Boerboels adored children. Two of my dogs started getting milk as soon as a newborn baby arrived. We would show them the baby and allow the dogs to smell it. Then they would lie next to the stroller when the baby was sleeping, and soon they would have milk. Neither of those dogs ever had puppies, and they were both spayed.

Still, when it comes to the protection of children, I tend to err on the side of caution. When the kids were playing, I would put my dog on a different side of the home to ensure no accidents happened if the dog thought it needed to protect anyone.

Puppy play dates

A great way to get dogs socialized is to allow them to have play dates with loads of different dogs. The more dogs, the better. If you are at all like me, you have friends with many different breeds and ages of dogs. It would be great to give your Boerboel the opportunity to interact with as many of them as possible.

Just like with children, socializing dogs with their peers is vital to teaching them proper behavior. And getting them to socialize with different ages and breeds opens their world up. As younger dogs, they learn to play with and befriend their own kind. It teaches them things like sharing and not being jealous when their owners' attention is divided.

Older dogs teach pups proper dog etiquette and manners, and playing with a wide variety of breeds helps them to not just interact with their own breed. When your Boerboel sees a breed that is unfamiliar, if he has been well socialized, his first reaction won't be aggression simply because he doesn't know what this strange little thing is.

If you don't have many other friends with pets, then places like puppy school and doggy daycare might be a way to get your dog the stimulation that he needs. Even an off-leash dog park is a great place to meet new canine companions. Just be careful of letting your own dog off-leash if he isn't completely clear on recall yet. I can't imagine a worst-case scenario than having your pup slip out of the gates of the park and get lost. A healthy sense of caution is important.

Puppy school

> "Do not go to dog parks. Problems can arise when other aggressive dogs cause a bad experience for your Boerboel pup. Instead, take your pup on a leash to parks and to stores where you can get him used to different sounds and places. Find good obedience classes from your local kennel clubs, with experienced dog people to help."
>
> BEVERLY SHUPE
> *Tall Oak's Kennel*

We all want to train our Boerboel puppies to the best of our abilities. But there really is no shame in needing some help. Boerboels can be really stubborn, and it is very possible that they just want to follow their own path. In such an event, it might be time to get help to correct the behavior before it really gets out of hand. And a puppy school is a great place to do that.

Even the best, most well-behaved dog can benefit from going to puppy school. It is a great place to socialize and learn from other dogs. And the same goes for you as a pet parent. There might be tricks and behavior that you never even thought to train your dog that you can both learn in puppy school.

Fiercely protective Boerboels

Boerboels are protective. They just are. Their first reaction in any situation will always be to protect their humans. So, making sure that they are comfortable in many situations is crucial to stop them from overreacting or showing protective tendencies at the wrong time.

Photo Courtesy of Christine Van Pelt

My first Boerboel was super sweet and adored her family. We, her children, were everything to her. There was no way that any stranger would get to me through that dog. She would give her life protecting me. But she also loved my parents.

To test and, yes, admittedly, tease her, my dad would sometimes act like he was going to spank us when she was close. Then she would take his hand and hold it; she would moan a little bit without letting go. She never broke his skin, never injured him, but she still protected us. The protective instinct can be channeled to ensure your Boerboel uses the right amount of force to protect without injuring someone.

At the same time, it is better to predict any problems that could come up and avoid them. For example, if you have a bunch of children over, it might be safer to take the dog out of the situation because he might not always understand what is screaming for play or what is real fear.

When you have people over, make sure the dog and the humans are comfortable with each other and introduce them to each other. Make sure your dog realizes that these visitors aren't any threats.

Making some small adjustments can ensure that your Boerboel never injures someone unintentionally simply because he wants to protect you.

CHAPTER 10

Living with a Giant Breed Dog

Bringing a Boerboel home is not like bringing home an average-sized dog. He is not going to lie quietly in the corner without being noticed. If anything, he is going to have a massive bed that takes up a big part of your living room.

A giant-breed dog is going to change your life in the best way possible for the most part. For me, there is nothing better than to snuggle with this giant dog that has so much power but that chooses to give you all of the love and loyalty it possesses. At the same time, having a giant dog does have some challenges you need to address.

Photo Courtesy of Armand Groenewald

Photo Courtesy
of Dana Voorhis

What it means for your home

Boerboels need space. In a small garden where my Yorkie can run around and play, a Boerboels would only be able to stretch out and lie down. Playing would be out of the question.

The same goes for your home. If the space doesn't allow you and a few people to be in it, then chances are you and your Boerboel won't fit either. Size is very much a factor when it comes to your Boerboel. They do eventually become older and settle down, becoming less energetic and more couch potatoes. But their size does not go away. You are going to have to take that size into account for however long you have the privilege of caring for your Boerboel.

There is the other added challenge of them being able to reach anything. For most dogs, if you don't want them eating your sandwich, then you just place it on the counter, and they can't reach it. But you won't have such luck with a Boerboel. There is a good chance that it will be able to reach pretty much anywhere you can reach. Once again, training is important.

If your Boerboel is going to live inside of your home, then you will need to make sure that there isn't a lot of clutter or any lack of space where the dog can move around in. To get to you, he might just walk all over your expensive ornaments, bumping into anything. And at a certain age, most Boerboel pups can seem very clumsy, so the problem will get worse.

There are no options of downsizing when you have a Boerboel. You need the space. But it will be worth every second. The love your dog gives will make up for any hassle.

Photo Courtesy of Christine Van Pelt

What it means for walks

Your giant Boerboel could end up walking you if you aren't careful. You need to make sure that you are sure of yourself and that the dog is equally sure of your leadership.

Do not let him start taking the lead. A grown Boerboel weighs the same as many men. He will be able to drag you if he catches you off guard. That is why it is so crucial to make sure that it never happens.

Living with a giant-breed dog just means that you need to be more in control at all times and more careful when

HELPFUL TIP
Big Dog, Big Exercise Needs

On average, dogs need between 30 minutes to two hours of exercise daily, depending on their breed and individual needs. Larger-breed dogs frequently need more exercise than their smaller canine relatives. Large-breed dogs also often enjoy swimming, a low-impact exercise that increases strength and is easy on the joints. Lack of adequate exercise can lead to troublesome behaviors such as inappropriate chewing and excessive barking.

it comes to walking your dog. It does not mean you need to be scared or that you need to keep your dog cooped up in the garden. A dog that is trained from puppyhood on will follow your lead, and he won't give you any problems.

Training and more training

> 66
>
> *"Boerboels are a very intelligent breed and are very easy to train. A soft approach is best as, despite their size and appearance, they are very sensitive to their owners and do not respond well to a firm hand. Training with treats always goes down well and will help keep their attention for longer periods."*
>
> MARK BEASLEY
> *Topguard Kennels*
>
> 99

It all comes down to training. If a dog is exposed to all sorts of situations, people, and animals from a young age, then none of those things will be unfamiliar to him, and none of those situations will cause unneeded stress that might cause a dangerous reaction. When you have taught your dog to listen to your commands, then he won't even realize that he is bigger than you and think that he doesn't have to listen.

Photo Courtesy of David Coppel

These are loving, beautiful dogs that, above all else, just want to please you. When they know how to do that, they would rather chew off their own leg than hurt you or displease you. Giant-breed dogs only become dangerous when they are unsure of a situation or when they are unsure of how you would want them to react.

That is why extensive training is so important. It might seem like a lot of effort at the start of your puppy's life with you, but it will pay off so much in the long run, and you will never have to worry about how your dog will react in certain situations. You will just know.

Photo Courtesy of Mikayla Hemphill

A healthy level of precaution

Even with all of the planning in the world and with all of the training, moments may come up that you have not walked your dog through. These are giant pups, and even if they are very unlikely to hurt anyone, you might not be able to stop your dog if he does try. Removing him from an uncomfortable situation, like when there are lots of children playing, when there are too many strangers in the house, or strangers that are moving around close to you is safer for the dog and humans alike.

People don't always read a situation correctly, and a dog relies on instinct that could be wrong. A healthy level of precaution does not mean you don't trust your dog; it is just being a good pet parent and making sure your animal remains safe.

HELPFUL TIP
Kid-Friendly Guard Dog?

Can a guard dog also be kid-friendly? The answer is yes, with a caveat. Early socialization is vital for any dog, especially if you want the dog to be comfortable around kids. Boerboels can become very protective of their family, including kids, but it's essential to make sure that this protective nature doesn't become too territorial. With adequate training and socialization, Boerboels can make excellent family dogs.

CHAPTER 11
Nutrition

Having a healthy diet is just as important to animals as it is to people. It can be challenging giving them what they need instead of just what they want.

In this chapter, we will explore some nutritional facts for Boerboels and help you on your path to keeping your dog healthy for as long as possible.

Why is nutrition so important?

Like many of us, dogs love to eat everything that is bad for them instead of eating what they need. But it can impact their entire life. Feeding your Boerboel too much or the wrong types of food could greatly impact his health. Young pups need the correct nutrition in order to become healthy adults.

Their immune systems can become compromised, and their growth and development can be stunted.

For adult dogs, proper nutrition remains crucial. Dogs that aren't fed a proper diet can get many different illnesses that are connected to their diet. Canine diabetes, loss of muscle tone, and even early death can all be caused by a diet that is unbalanced.

It is very important to make sure your dog is getting a proper diet, but it can be really confusing. There are so many products out there. Additionally, older Boerboels have different nutritional require-ments than younger Boerboels. A dog that is very active has very dif-ferent requirements than a dog that is lazier. A more energetic dog might

Photo Courtesy of Estie van Zyl

need a diet that is higher in protein, while such a diet could just make a dog with average activity obese. There is a lot to think about.

That is why much of what we are going to talk about in this chapter are general ideas. A vet can give you a much better idea of what your dog specifically needs. They might also know about the kind of food that is available in the area. Don't be shy, and speak to your vet if you are unsure.

Managing obesity in Boerboels

Obesity is a big problem that Boerboels can have. They are very active when they are young but can tend to get lazy as they age. And with that, they can pick up weight. It is much harder to get your overweight dog to lose weight than it is to just control his diet and exercise from the start. But how do you know when a Boerboel is starting to become obese in the first place? According to vets, you need to be able to easily feel a dog's ribs. You should never be able to see the ribs, but you should be able to feel them without pressing too hard. Your dog's abdomen should also be slightly tucked in from the chest.

Exercise and portion control

> "A good steady exercise regime is the best way to keep Boerboels fit. Hill walking is great for the rear legs and top line; swimming is also great as it's low stress for the joints and most Boerboels love the water. Try to stay away from too much prolonged running. Although the Boerboel is a very fit and functional breed for such a large dog, too much heavy, long-distance running day in and day out will eventually have an effect on the animal's joints."
>
> MARK BEASLEY
> *Topguard Kennels*

The first rule in making sure that a Boerboel doesn't become obese is to ensure that he keeps moving. If you aren't a person that is inclined to be active, it can be easy to let walks and other activities slide. Trust me, I understand. I have a chronic illness that is very painful. After a long day of work, it is just so much easier to stretch out in front of the television and cuddle up with your pooch. But if your dog's daily walk is the only time that he is active, then it is even more crucial that you don't let that time slide. It is good for his muscles, his bones, and his overall health and happiness.

Another mistake that some new pet parents make is when it comes to portion control. You can easily get into the habit of feeding your dog a certain amount of food when he is a pup, and then when he is finished growing, you keep feeding him the same amount of food.

Adult dogs need much less food than puppies do. No one wants their dog to go hungry, but it can be just as unhealthy to overfeed your dog. If your dog keeps licking his bowl or going back, then you might try to give him a little bit more to see if he is then satisfied. But some dogs never learn, and they will always keep eating. You will need to be a little bit hard-hearted and do what is healthy for your dog rather than what he would prefer.

Most good foods have a portion per age and weight indication on the packaging, so that is a good place to start to figure out how much your dog should be eating.

Different foods available

We all want to give our dogs the best foods, but it can be really hard to know what that is. There is wet dog food, there is raw dog food, and there is a diet of only kibble. Each has its own pros and cons. And each dog is different. Some might be willing to eat a diet of kibble, but others just won't eat it at all. Let's get into more detail about the various kinds of dog food available.

KIBBLE

Kibble is normally a mix of dog food that is dried and made by machine. There is a wide variety of kibble available. Cheaper versions use less expensive and lower-grade ingredients. Some versions that are sold privately aren't inspected at all. They can put in pretty much whatever they want, and you would never know. Some of the very cheap options just won't make the cut in giving your dog the nutrients he needs to stay healthy.

If you do decide to go with kibble, a vet-approved diet would be preferable. Vet-approved brands are monitored closely, and they contain better ingredients. They are fully balanced meals. Note that many of those brands can be very expensive, and with a Boerboel-sized appetite, this can be a pretty pricey option.

Still, buying your dog a food that is a bit more expensive will help you save money in the long run because proper nutrition will help your dog stay healthy and will help to limit vet bills.

Photo Courtesy
of Isabel Cisneros

My vet told me that it is really good for dogs to eat some kibble because harder food helps with dental health and keeps their teeth clean. If you do go in a softer food direction, you will have to use other options to help with dental health.

Kibble is also the easiest food to buy in larger quantities and to store safely. The biggest problem is making sure that insects like ants don't get in it, but storing the kibble in an airtight container should be enough to take care of that.

That said, there are many people who believe that kibble isn't as healthy as some of the alternatives because it is more processed.

WET DOG FOOD

Then there is wet food that comes in cans. Again, there are many options available. Vet-approved food is better if you can afford it. You might decide to give your dog one wet food meal a day and give him kibble as a snack in between.

Wet food that comes in cans is higher in protein and fat and is thus easier to eat and digest. Wet dog food is great for smaller dogs and also dogs that have some health issues. For example, a dog that has just had surgery could do better on wet food because it is easier to digest. A dog that is a picky eater is more likely to start eating wet food than dry. Dogs digest this food quicker, so they run through the energy given by wet food quicker. Small dogs don't need as much energy as big dogs do to function, and this is another reason that wet food works better for smaller dogs rather than big dogs like Boerboels.

It is better to put a dog that needs to gain weight on a wet food diet, but that means the flip side is true too. Boerboels tend to gain weight easily, so giving them wet food exclusively might not be the best choice. It is fine for the occasional treat, but another form of food is better for them.

RAW FOOD DIET

One more trend today is feeding dogs a raw food diet. Some companies deliver a raw food portion right to your door. Some believe raw food diets are really great for dogs' health and say you can see it in their coats and how healthy they stay.

Of course, it would be good to check out these companies and find out what their reputations are before you use them. Other pet owners could be a vital source of information if you do decide to make use of their services.

The problem with a raw food diet is that it can be difficult to store and to work with. Cross-contamination is a big problem, and it can cause problems for both humans and dogs with things like salmonella.

The biggest part of the raw food diet is meat. Protein and fat are important for the energy levels and health of your dog. You need to make sure your Boerboel doesn't get too much fat but still gets enough to keep active.

Photo Courtesy
of Bronwyn Du Toit

It is possible to feed your dog homemade raw dog food. It does take effort, but by making it at home, you know exactly what your dog is eating. You have complete control.

But if that sounds like too much of a commitment, a good raw food company that supplies the food is a really great option. Some prepack the exact portion for each meal, and you only need to take one portion out of the fridge to feed your dog.

THE CONCLUSION

In the end, each dog is different. You might really want to serve your Boerboel a certain type of food that you have put a lot of research into, and then he might just not want to eat it. It happens.

Most Boerboels aren't really picky eaters, but there are always exceptions when they will just refuse to eat what you give them. You will learn your own dog's tastes and have to adapt accordingly.

The most important part is to make sure that the food you choose is appropriate for your dog's age and activity level. Puppies might not be able to digest adult food, and puppy food might be too calorie-rich for an adult dog.

Most high-end dog foods, whether wet food or dry food, have different options, such as for senior dogs or for dogs that are having trouble with their joints or other health problems. There are also foods available for weight control, for instance.

The biggest considerations when deciding what type of food to feed your dog is the price you can pay and the needs of your dog. If you are very active, and you take your dog with you when you exercise, then you will need to give him a much higher protein diet than someone who only walks a dog once a day.

HEALTH CHECK
Hypothyroidism and Weight Gain

Hypothyroidism can affect any dog breed but may be more common in Boerboels. It's caused when the thyroid gland doesn't produce adequate thyroxine, a hormone that controls your dog's metabolism. If you notice that your Boerboel has put on some extra weight despite a healthy exercise regime and diet, hypothyroidism could be the cause. Weight gain is just one of the symptoms of this disease. Sluggishness, decreased appetite, hair loss, and flaky skin are other symptoms to look out for. Don't hesitate to talk to your vet about possible hypothyroidism, as it's usually simple to treat and can negatively impact your dog's quality of life if left untreated.

When table scraps can become dangerous

The puppy dog eyes making you feel guilty whenever you eat something without sharing can be brutal. But there are times when it can just be dangerous to feed your dog table scraps. There are many foods that humans can eat but that can be toxic to your pup.

- Xylitol, found in things like some baked goods and diet foods, can drop your dog's blood sugar and can even cause liver failure and eventual death.

- Lots of fruit pits and seeds can be really toxic, like apple and cherry pits. They contain cyanide and can also get lodged in a dog's digestive tract and cause blockages in the intestines.

- Avocados can be toxic to many different animals, including dogs. Persin can be found in the bark of the tree, the leaves of the plant, the seeds, and the fruit. Eating this can cause vomiting and diarrhea in dogs. Most of the time, it won't be fatal in dogs, but it can make them really sick, and they could die due to dehydration.

- Chocolate contains theobromine, a compound that dogs can't process as quickly as humans can. In small quantities, it would probably only make a dog as big as a Boerboel sick. But larger quantities with higher cocoa content can cause internal bleeding, tremors, seizures, and even heart attacks. It really isn't worth it to give your dog the piece of chocolate it is begging for.

- Garlic and onions contain thiosulfate that causes damage to the red blood cells, making your dog anemic and causing his red blood cells to rupture. You might not immediately realize that your dog is getting sick from these foods, but he could be sustaining internal damage.

- Grapes and raisins can cause serious kidney injury and even sudden onset kidney failure, so a dog stops producing urine, which can be fatal.

- Alcohol is really toxic to dogs because it can lower their respiratory rate and make their breathing labored.

If you really want to give your dog some of your table scraps, but you aren't sure, then a quick internet search could give you peace of mind and keep your dog safe. It is important to remember that dogs don't digest all substances the same way as we do. Things that are fine for human consumption might be really dangerous to your best friend. The moral of the story is to make sure that any table scraps you give your dog are safe to eat, and don't give him too much since that can be dangerous too.

CHAPTER 12

Grooming your Boerboel

You can't exactly just pop your Boerboel in your car and drive him over to the groomer every other week. Still, his grooming is just as important as it would be for any other animal.

Photo Courtesy of Wendy Lehr

Shedding

A Boerboel sheds a moderate amount. But when you have a massive dog, even a moderate amount can result in a lot of hair flying around all over the place.

If you brush your dog about once a week, that will remove most excess loose hair. The best brushes for this are a soft-bristle brush, a hound glove, or grooming mitt.

The bonus is that if you start brushing your dog from a young age, then he will come to expect it. And not only will he tolerate it, but he will enjoy spending time with you and getting the extra attention. What dog doesn't love being petted? And with a glove, that is all you are basically doing. It will also keep your dog's coat shiny and looking its best.

> ### HELPFUL TIP
> **The Perfect Brush**
>
>
> Boerboels are relatively low maintenance in the grooming department, but they still need regular brushing to keep their coat looking top-notch. Weekly brushing is a good frequency to shoot for with this breed. Grooming gloves are a popular choice for the Boerboel's short hair. Gloves remove excess hair, distribute the natural oils from your dog's skin, and supposedly feel like a massage for your canine companion. Other good options for Boerboels are pin brushes and bristle brushes.

If some puppy glitter does make its way onto your clothing, then the hair is easily removed with a sticky roller. That said, if your dog does shed a lot, then you should take notice. This can be an early sign that he is having some sort of health crisis. Or it could just come back to nutrition. A dog that isn't getting enough nutrients will shed more, and he won't be as shiny as a well-nourished Boerboel. An observant pet parent can notice a health problem before it becomes serious just by taking into account a Boerboel's physical appearance.

Boerboels and bath time

One of my Boerboels hated baths so much that it was a two-person job. We would have to make sure that she didn't see us running the water or getting the dog shampoo ready. If she did see it, she would bolt into a dog kennel, and it was absolutely game over. We could not budge her.

Then one of us would have to sit with her and hold her while the other person brought everything we needed closer. I would have to sit and hold her while another person did the washing. I would be soaked in the end, but at least my dog would be clean.

A big shower might have made life much easier, but we did not have access to one that would fit our Boerboel. So, we used a bucket of warm water and another to rinse. Where I live is very hot, so there is no danger of the dog getting sick from being bathed outdoors, but that is something to consider when bathing your pup.

The latest thought is that you should bathe your dog around every four weeks to make sure you don't dry out its skin, but it all depends on how dirty the dog is. If he plays in mud, then you are obviously going to need to bathe him more often.

Teaching dogs to take baths as soon as you get them is important and will help you when they are older.

Photo Courtesy of Christopher Mcelhinny

Things you need to bathe your dog:

- Buckets of warm water, or, if it is a really warm day, then a garden hose set to small spray can work too
- Dog shampoo—human shampoo can dry out a dog's skin
- A washcloth
- A dog brush
- A drying towel
- Possibly a hair dryer, depending on the temperature

To bathe your Boerboel:

1. Start by getting your dog's fur wet. Be careful not to spray water into his ears since dogs' ears are shaped differently from our own, and they struggle to get water out of their ear canals. This can lead to ear infections. If you do have a dog that is prone to ear infections, then it might be better to plug his ears with dog earplugs or even cotton wool for extra protection. When wetting the dog's face, I like to hold his ears closed with one hand to make sure no water goes in.

2. When your dog is wet, then it is time to lather him with dog shampoo and wash him all over. Stay away from the eyes and ears.

3. Rinse the dog off. Make very sure that the soap is completely cleaned off. If you do leave some soap, it can lead to your Boerboel having dry skin and itchiness.

4. Using the washcloth, wipe the dog's eyes to clean away any discharge that might have built up. Also, use the cloth to clean inside the dog's ears. Cleaning with a cloth is safer to make sure no water gets in there.

5. If it is really hot, then you can just dry the dog with a towel. But if it is colder, it might be better to dry your dog with a hairdryer. Also, if you do take the extra time to dry your dog completely, then it is less likely that your newly cleaned pup will go roll in grass or dirt with wet hair and be covered in sand right away, needing another bath.

6. Brushing your dog down after he is dry can help to clean away any loose hair that has been further loosened by the bath. It can also help to keep your dog's coat shiny. Brushing was my dogs' favorite part of bath time.

7. An extra step I like to add is to give my dog a nice snack after he has been good for his bath. This ends things on a high note and gives him positive feelings about bath time.

Dental care

If you start training your dog as a puppy, it's actually pretty easy to teach him to allow you to brush his teeth. Make sure you use canine toothpaste, not human toothpaste, which is toxic to dogs. At first, just take a little bit of toothpaste and put it on the dog's lip. Let him get used to it. Then you can use your toothpaste-coated finger and rub the dog's teeth. Eventually, you can use a baby toothbrush or a special dog toothbrush available at pet shops. Boerboels have big teeth, so it is not hard to make sure you get to all of them.

Take it easy at first. If you notice your dog is done, then stop. Don't overdo it, and make him hate the experience. And always give a healthy treat afterward. Generally, vets say that you should brush your dog's at least once or twice a week, but if you can do it even more regularly, that's even better.

Choose a calm time to brush your Boerboel's teeth. Before bed might be the best time to do it. Helping your dog get into a routine is important. Choose a spot where you can see well and where your pup is really comfortable.

1. When you are just starting out, the best way to begin is by just touching the teeth and gums without the toothbrush. This will help your dog get used to having his mouth handled. With a well-socialized dog, this step shouldn't be a problem.

2. Touch your dog's teeth with the brush. Then just touch the brush to the front side and back teeth on both the top and bottom parts of the teeth. If your dog tolerates this at all, then praise him very enthusiastically. You can even reward him.

3. Next, give your dog some toothpaste. At first, you can just allow him to lick some of the toothpaste off your finger. Dog toothpastes generally taste pretty good, so this could get your Boerboel excited.

4. Then add paste onto the brush. You don't need loads of toothpaste, but adding more might give your dog an incentive for allowing you to continue.

5. Start brushing. The best way is to start at the top and the front. Hold your dog's lip to make sure you don't hurt him accidentally. Brush the front teeth and then try to continue brushing to the back of the mouth but only the front side.

6. Hold the bottom lip, and again, start from the front and move to the back.

7. Brush the sides and back, and eventually, if possible, brush the back of the teeth.

8. Make sure that the dog stays comfortable. Especially in the beginning, when you are just starting out, you need to stop when your dog is tensing up. Try to go further the next time you brush.

9. Be super generous with your praise. This is not something that is fun for your dog, but when he tolerates it, it is because he wants to please you.

Photo Courtesy of Nadine Beattie Beattie Boerboels

Nail care

> "Nails, nails, nails! Your life will be much more pleasant if you teach your Boerboel to let his nails be Dremmeled as a baby. Wrestling 150 pounds of unhappy dog is not fun, and no one wants to go to the vet every time nails need to be done!"
>
> KATE NICHOLSON
> *Wilby Boerboels*

Dog nails can be trimmed around once every two weeks, but this also greatly depends on the activity of your pup. If he goes on hikes or walks on rugged terrain, then he might wear his nails down naturally, and you can do it less frequently. If you leave your dog's nails to grow too long, it can be really bad for your dog since it can be painful, and it can affect how he walks. A big dog's nails need to be trimmed as soon as they touch the floor.

You need nail trimmers that are made for a big dog's nails. Guillotine-style nail trimmers or scissor-style trimmers can both work as long as they are made for big dogs. Or you could use a nail grinder for large dogs. The Dremel grinder, for example, works really well for large dogs since it picks up some of the dust. Some dogs just don't like the noise and vibration, so if you do want to use that option, get the pup used to it from a young age. It allows you a bit more control since you grind off a piece at a time. Have styptic powder on hand in case you cut too deeply and cut the quick in your dog's nail.

Some Boerboels have lighter-colored nails, while others have black nails. If you are lucky enough to have a dog with light nails, then this makes things much easier.

Inside the light nail, you will see that there is a pink spot just above the curve. This is a bundle of nerves called the quick, and you really want to avoid cutting it. That will hurt your pup, and it will bleed. If that does happen, then you can press some styptic powder into the nail to stop the bleeding.

How to trim the nails:

- Sit comfortably with your dog and start touching his feet to get him ready. If you have handled your dog's paws since he was young, then he will be used to his paws being touched, and trimming his nails will be easier.

101

- For some Boerboels, you can sit on a small stool with them in front of you between your legs facing forward. Then you can pick up their paw while still holding them somewhat still with your legs. For dogs that are more nervous and try to move, you might need the help of a second person.

- Examine the nail for the quick.

- Hold your Boerboel's paw firmly, and with the other hand, cut his nail just below the quick. If he has dark nails, then cut a piece at a time until they are short enough. When you start to see a circle appear on the pieces of nail that are being cut off, then you are getting too close to the quick, and you should stop trimming.

- Alternatively, start to grind the nail, being very careful not to grind too deeply too quickly. It can happen easily, so going slow is key.

- Check to make sure that there are no nails that are bleeding, and press in some styptic powder on the nails that might be cut too deeply.

For a dog that does not want to cooperate, you can ask someone else to hold him while you trim the nails. Remember to use lots of praise and treats to keep the dog's attention and make the experience positive.

If you are really nervous about trimming your dog's nails, then you could always take him to the vet, as they don't normally charge too much to do this. This is a crucial part of keeping your dog healthy.

Eye and ear care

None of the Boerboels I had ever had any issues with ear infections. But they don't have especially large ears, and their ears are floppy, making for a soft and warm environment where wax and infections can potentially build up. There are lots of wonderful products like ear wipes that can easily be used once a week to clean the insides of your dog's ears.

If you see your dog scratching his ear more than usual, or he suddenly shakes his head more than normal, then it is a good indication that an ear infection could be in the works. You need to get the dog to a vet if you suspect anything because an ear infection can be really painful, and there is almost no chance that it will clear up on its own.

Some dogs might need more or less regular ear cleanings as they will naturally have more or less wax build-up. You will get to know your own dog.

There isn't a lot of upkeep needed for a Boerboel's eyes. They don't have a lot of discharge or buildup. Cleaning your dog's face during bath time should keep his eyes clean enough. If you do have a pup that has a bit more eye discharge than normal, then you can keep that under control by wiping his face with a warm cloth every few days.

If your dog that never has eye discharge or red eyes suddenly does, then you need to have him checked since he probably has an eye infection.

Finding a groomer who will work with a Boerboel

Boerboels don't really need haircuts, but it might just be easier to get a groomer to come in and give your dog his bath and nail trim and a dental cleaning. But if you live in an area where Boerboels aren't very popular, then it might be difficult to get a groomer that is familiar with the breed.

Groomers might even be scared of trying to groom such a big breed. And if it is a groomer that comes to you, then they might have to adjust the way they work with these dogs. I have a groomer that comes to my house.

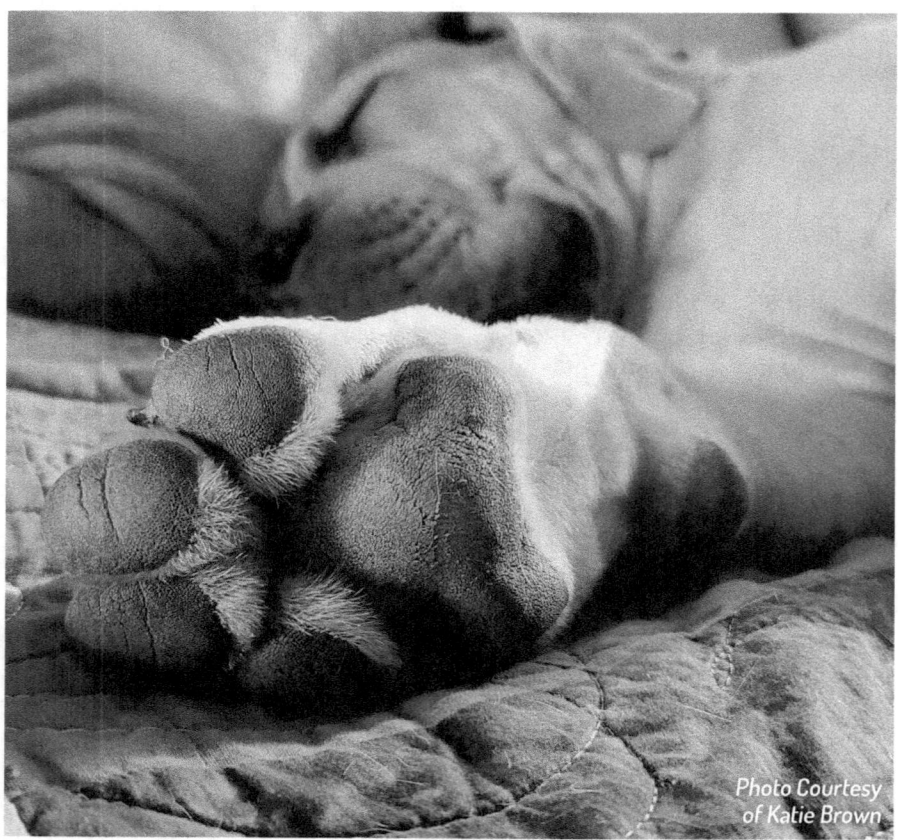

Photo Courtesy
of Katie Brown

For my groomer, it is impossible to get a Boerboel into the mobile grooming salon. They have to groom the dog outside. This is fine if you are comfortable with it and the weather is nice enough. But that would be one of the questions you need to ask when choosing a groomer.

Give any groomer a heads-up on how big your dog is when you make the appointment. That way, they can make arrangements, and they can also tell you if they aren't comfortable with grooming such a big dog.

The easiest way to go would probably be to start working with a groomer when your dog is a young puppy. That way, your dog will be used to getting groomed, and your groomer will know your dog and be used to him by the time he is fully grown, making life much easier for everyone.

Most of these groomers can come and do a full groom where they cut the dog's hair, something that is not really needed for a Boerboel, give them baths, trim their nails, clean the eyes and ears, and anything else you require of them. Some only specialize in smaller dogs, while others are willing to work with bigger dogs. For Boerboels, you will mostly need them to come out and give him a bath and eye and ear clean, plus getting his nails trimmed. Again, you don't really need a groomer with a Boerboel. If you have the time and energy to do these jobs yourself, then you can completely do that. But having someone you know for the times when life gets busy is always a good option to have.

They do dental cleaning, but these are generally just brushing the dog's teeth and giving them something to treat stinky breath. It is not the type of cleaning that you get at the vet. If you are already brushing his teeth regularly, then it is probably about the same level of cleaning that you are already giving him. So, if you have noticed a stronger odor from his mouth and a lot of buildup on the teeth, then taking him to the groomer won't be enough; he needs to be checked at the vet.

The price of groomers can vary greatly, even just from one suburb to another. In my area, the average price is around $30 per full groom. But in just a 10-minute radius from me, it can go up and down as much as $10 both ways. Driving a bit further might be worth it to you, and shopping around is important.

But the most important part of finding a great groomer is finding one that your dog is comfortable with. If your dog is normally completely fine with being bathed but they are really nervous at the groomers, then it might be a sign that you need to look for someone else. Of course, if you know that your dog always hates a bath, it could also be a simple case of knowing what comes next. You will know your own dog and be able to read their body language.

CHAPTER 13
Health Basics

None of us want our dogs to become ill. Sadly, one fact about having a pet is that it will eventually become sick at some point. Being prepared for as many situations as possible can really help you. Your imagination can, at times, be much worse than reality. And when you know what to look out for, you can get your Boerboel help much quicker.

Photo Courtesy of Nico Kilian

Puppy illnesses to look out for

Losing a dog when he is still a puppy has to be one of the saddest things a dog parent can go through. Sadly, there are a number of illnesses that can kill a young dog very easily. That is why getting your pup vaccinated is so incredibly important. Even if he does pick up some of these illnesses, a vaccinated puppy is more likely to pull through. The following are some of the most common puppy illnesses that you need to look out for.

- **Parvovirus**

Commonly known as parvo, this illness, caused by the parvovirus, is really contagious. It is very common and can spread through direct contact with another sick dog or contact with a contaminated object. That is why it is really important to sanitize everything if you lose a puppy to this illness. Otherwise, if you get another puppy, it can get sick too.

In some areas, parvo is colloquially known as canine cat flu, and it can easily kill your pup. The good news is when a vaccinated dog gets it, the effects of the disease are almost always much milder. I had one dog that passed away from this illness, and let me tell you, it is really horrible to watch. A combination of my puppy being too young to be fully vaccinated yet, plus a vet that didn't seem to care combined to create a really sad ending.

Parvo attacks pups aged between 12 weeks, and it can still infect dogs up to three years of age. Puppies normally get their first vaccination against parvo when they are around six to eight weeks old, and then they get it again every three weeks until they are around four months old. It should be noted that your vet could recommend that your pup get more or fewer vaccinations.

Signs of parvo normally start with a fever. If you see any signs of fever, then you should monitor your dog closely. For example, if it is a cold day and your dog is panting, then it could be a danger sign. Dogs are very contagious to other canines at this point, but they won't transfer the illness to humans. After being sick for a few days, your dog may start to experience vomiting and bloody diarrhea. This is very dangerous since puppies can really quickly become weak and dehydrated.

Puppies with parvo will normally be hospitalized for dehydration and possible sepsis, something that I didn't know when my pup got sick. When the vet sent him home after giving him IV fluids, I allowed it, and I still regret not taking my puppy somewhere else for a second opinion. Normally puppies can take up to seven days to get better with the proper medication.

Please vaccinate your dog against this illness.

- **Distemper**

Caused by the paramyxovirus, this is a really horrible disease that once again can be prevented by vaccinating your pup. After only two vaccinations, dogs are immune to the disease. The most common way dogs get distemper is through the respiratory droplets spread when a sick dog coughs or sneezes or when dogs use the same water or food bowls. The disease can also be transmitted through infected urine, blood, or saliva.

Even when your puppy does survive this disease, it can lie dormant for years. Then, when he is older, he can become sick again. Only then, the illness is even worse and leads to neurological problems and even serious seizures.

Initially, your pup may look like he only has a cold. He can show signs like sneezing and eye discharge. Many pet parents might not think that it is a big deal, and by the time they realize that their dog needs to see the vet, he is seriously ill already. By then, the dog could have a lot of discharge from the eyes and nose, have a high fever, and might have pneumonia. Distemper can lead to neurological problems and brain damage that can be fatal.

It can take weeks for a puppy to recover from distemper and even after being in hospital for a long time, he'll need to have medicine that supports the respiratory tract for a while afterward.

- **Kennel Cough**

Kennel cough, which is not confined to kennels and is highly contagious, is caused by bacterial infections or canine parainfluenza, airborne diseases that are really infectious and can lead to pneumonia. The first signs are normally a puppy that is more lethargic, doesn't have a normal appetite, and is feverish. He may get bronchitis or pneumonia.

If your puppy starts to cough, then it is probably a good idea to get it checked out. Vaccinated pups can still develop kennel cough, but they won't get as sick, and their symptoms will be milder.

Normally, mild cases of kennel cough are only treated with a lot of rest. Antibiotics might be needed if a dog is really sick. Since it is a viral infection, the medication won't help with the illness itself, but the antibiotics will help to avoid any secondary infections.

Most kennels will not take a dog that has not already been fully vaccinated against kennel cough.

- **Adenovirus**

This is not an illness that is seen a lot any more thanks to effective vaccines, but this virus causes canine hepatitis. It is spread directly from dog to dog. With many dogs vaccinated against it, transmission has become less.

It is spread through infected feces or urine or through any directly transferred respiratory secretions. Normally, it starts with vomiting and diarrhea, and dogs can eventually develop jaundice. Treatment for adenovirus normally includes antibiotics and fluids and support to make sure a pup gets enough nutrients.

- **Leptospirosis**

Your puppy can pick up leptospirosis from contaminated water or contact with infected urine. Then, this bacterial illness can affect the kidneys and liver. The symptoms of the bacterial infection can be very much like the flu. Your pup may vomit, have a fever, or be very lethargic.

The condition can be treated with antibiotics.

Though the vaccine for this illness is really effective, not all clinics automatically vaccinate dogs for this condition. Talk to your vet about this vaccine and whether or not it is needed for your pup.

- **Vomiting and Diarrhea**

Vomiting and diarrhea can be signs of many problems, including intestinal parasites. Other times they are merely a sign that your pup ate something he probably shouldn't have. Most of the time, the symptoms will get better on their own. But if your dog is vomiting and/or has diarrhea that doesn't get better after 12 hours, have him checked out by a vet.

The most important thing when your pup is vomiting is to make sure he is staying hydrated. He will probably not want to eat, but you should offer him food often and ensure he takes in fluids.

Other diseases to look out for

Other medical conditions you should watch your dog for include:

- **Eye disease**

If your dog has any type of abnormal eye secretions, any discoloration, or any masses near the eye, get him checked out by a vet to ensure there is nothing seriously wrong. Most eye infections can be treated with eye drops.

- **Ear disease**

Ear infection is another common illness that can occur in dogs. Getting an ear infection can be easily treated, but it can also be really painful, and it won't go away on its own. Early signs include excessive head shaking and scratching. The ear can also have some discharge and a foul odor. There can be red skin on the outside of your dog's ear, but if the infection is deep in the ear canal, you might not be able to see any major physical signs on the ear.

Normally ear drops will do the trick, but a dog with a severe infection might need some antibiotics too.

If your dog is prone to ear infections, it is important to make sure that he doesn't get water in his ears from swimming or bathing. There are products on the market that you can put into your puppy's ear after contact with water that will help to dry out his ears and prevent ear infections.

- **Arthritis**

Arthritis is another big risk, especially to bigger dogs like Boerboels. It is when your dog's joints can become really swollen and painful. It can be caused by autoimmune illness or by a dog's size due to excessive pressure on his joints. Arthritis is another reason to ensure that your dog does not become overweight, but it can still be a big challenge in large-breed dogs.

The three main types of arthritis that affect dogs are:

OSTEOARTHRITIS

This can be caused by aging, but it can also be caused by other conditions, such as the damage that hip and elbow dysplasia can cause in younger dogs. Dogs that are put through obstacle training and strenuous exercise can also experience this form of arthritis in later life. Dogs that are overweight are also very likely to experience this type of arthritis because their joints are put under undue stress.

AUTOIMMUNE DISEASE

In both humans and dogs, autoimmune disease can be a big cause of arthritis. It happens when a dog's own antibodies, which are supposed to protect him, start to attack the healthy tissue around the joints. It is important to get the dog treatment for the underlying condition because if that is not treated, the pain in the joints will remain, and it can cause serious damage. Treatments include steroids and anti-inflammatory drugs plus immunosuppressants.

ARTHRITIS CAUSED BY OTHER ILLNESSES

Then there are other illnesses that can cause swelling of joints. Things like Lyme disease and other infections can show up as arthritis. Once the underlying infection is treated, the arthritis should clear up. Scrapes or cuts that allow bacteria to enter the bloodstream can be another cause of this type of arthritis.

It can be hard to see the symptoms of arthritis in dogs because they generally try to hide any mild pain and continue on with their routines as

Photo Courtesy of De Ron Arneaud

normal. But when left untreated, the pain will increase, and symptoms will get worse. Noticing the problem as quickly as possible will ensure that your dog doesn't remain in pain for longer than necessary and will ensure that any illnesses are treated before they cause major damage. Some things to look out for:

- A dog that is unwilling or unable to do the same amount of exercise that he is used to doing
- Hesitation when climbing stairs or on furniture
- Resting more than is usual for your dog
- Any signs of pain when you touch him
- Your dog seems stiff in the morning but seems to feel better as the day goes on
- Swollen joints
- Weight gain

- Your dog is walking in a strange way or has a strange posture
- Any limbs that show signs of being lame or hard to use
- Your dog is not eating as he normally does
- General signs that your dog is not acting like himself

Because there are so many underlying causes of arthritis, it is important to get your dog diagnosed before any treatment starts. Things like X-rays, blood tests, and physical examinations will allow the vet to assess your dog for arthritis and, if it exists, to determine its origin.

Then the vet can decide on a treatment plan. Physiotherapy, medical treatment for the illness, and treatment for the pain, plus possible adjustments to diet, will be combined to keep your dog healthy and pain-free.

Talk to your vet about possible supplements to help prevent or delay the onset of arthritis. Never treat your dog without a proper diagnosis first.

Vaccinations

A puppy needs his first vaccines at six to eight weeks old, and then he will need two more vaccines in four-week intervals. The core vaccines are given more than one at a time, and they help prevent various illnesses. A few have to be given by law, like the rabies vaccine. If there are any outbreaks in your area, your vet will also advise you to vaccinate your pup against certain illnesses.

You will probably need to get your pup vaccinated at six, 12, and 16 weeks of age, though, generally, puppies are given their first vaccines before they leave the breeder.

The price of vaccines differs a lot in different areas, as do vet prices. On average, the cost for the core vaccines and visits is around $75 to $100. Then, if you need extra vaccines like the rabies vaccines, that will add around $15 to $20 to your vet bill.

After your dog's vaccines are up to date, then you only need to take him for top-ups once a year.

Spaying and neutering

A puppy normally gets spayed or neutered at around four to six months of age. Many breeder contracts expect you to spay or neuter your dog, and in reality, it is better for your dog, as many types of cancers can be prevented when you spay and neuter. Additionally, for female dogs, things like bloody discharge, howling, and erratic behavior can be prevented by spaying. For males, neutering stops behavior like marking their territory, breaking out of the yard to search for a mate, and fighting with other male dogs.

That said, new research has found that spaying or neutering a dog at a young age can lead to joint illnesses later in life. The research suggests that sex hormones can help with the development of a stronger skeletal system. For dogs as big and as heavy as a Boerboel, this can be a real risk and should factor into your decision of when to spay or neuter your dog. Speak to your vet and get their opinion on the subject.

There is no denying that it is better to get your Boerboel spayed or neutered, but waiting until he is about a year old could be better.

Tick and flea treatment

Depending on where you live and the environment where you take your dog for walks, you might need to regularly use tick and flea treatment. If you walk in places with long grass or are in a more rural environment, your dog could come into contact with these pests, though fleas and ticks can also be found elsewhere. Ticks are active year-round, so don't assume that weather conditions like frost have killed off these little pests. They might still be active and looking for a host to feed on.

WHAT ARE TICKS?

Ticks are ugly little bugs that have a sticky substance that helps them to stick to the skin of both humans and animals. They also burrow into the skin. They feed on blood, and the area can become red and irritated. If you don't get ticks off in time, they can feed on so much of your dog's blood that he can become anemic. They also transmit different bacteria and viruses that can make your dog really sick.

Something like tick bite fever can be deadly for both humans and dogs. That is why it is so crucial to not only check your dog and remove any ticks as soon as possible but also to prevent ticks from getting on your dog in the first place.

Ticks can be black, brown, or tan, and they have eight legs. Sometimes they just look like a little dot on your dog's skin. Though some are only about the size of the head of a pin, they can still do a lot of damage.

Photo Courtesy
of Kenzie Christopher

WHAT ARE FLEAS?

These bugs can jump from host to host, and they produce 50 eggs a day. It can seem like your dog doesn't have them, and then suddenly, overnight, there are loads of fleas on your dog and in your house. Fleas can cause serious skin irritation and discomfort to your dog and you. It's best to prevent them in the first place.

HOW TO TELL IF YOUR DOG HAS TICKS AND HOW TO TREAT THEM

Ticks are pretty easy to spot. At first, they are just small black dots on the skin. But then, eventually, as they feed on the dog's blood, they grow and can become big black masses that sit on top of your dog's skin. Check your Boerboel's entire body, including the groin, between the toes, all around the legs, inside the ears, where it is warm and dark, and around the chin and neck. A Boerboel has some loose skin around the neck areas, and this is another great spot for ticks to hide, so check in the skin folds too.

You need to be very thorough when removing a tick from your dog because if you leave behind any of the tick's body that is still buried in your dog, this can still lead to illness. To remove a tick:

- First, get some gloves. Ticks are really dangerous for humans, too, so you don't want to risk contact with your own skin.

- Use tweezers or special tick removers that you can find at your local pet shop. Pinch the tick as close to your dog's skin as you possibly can without hurting your Boerboel.

- If you are using tweezers, pull the tick out slowly and in a straight motion to ensure that you don't break off a piece, leaving the rest still embedded in your dog. When using a tick remover, press the remover against your Boerboel's skin near the tick and then slide the notch under the tick, pulling it free.

- Clean the wound that is left on the skin with antiseptic cream and keep an eye on the area for a few days to make sure that it doesn't get infected. If it does get irritated or infected, get it checked by the vet.

- Keep the tick in isopropyl alcohol and write down the date that you removed it. Then if your dog does get sick, the vet can test the tick for diseases.

- Make sure to wash your hands very thoroughly and clean the tweezers with isopropyl alcohol afterward.

Two of the biggest dangers from tick bites are Lyme disease and Rocky Mountain spotted fever.

LYME DISEASE

This comes from bacteria that the black-legged tick can transmit. As dangerous as Lyme disease can be to humans, it can also be very dangerous to dogs. It can take a long time for dogs to start showing signs of Lyme disease. Some of the symptoms include:

- Fever
- Swollen joints
- Limping or lameness in some joints. This can shift to different legs and could come and go.
- Kidney problems, such as more frequent urinating
- Just generally being stiffer and seeming uncomfortable or in pain
- Drooling more than usual
- Depression
- Lack of normal appetite

Blood tests will be able to detect Lyme disease in dogs. The vet will also probably do tests to see how it has affected your dog. Lyme disease can damage the heart, the kidneys, and even the nervous system. That is why it is so important to get your dog checked if you suspect any issues coming from a tick bite. When Lyme disease is diagnosed early enough, it can be treated with antibiotics. It can get pretty costly. A four-week course could cost up to $800 or more. Added to that, you have the price for blood tests and for vet consults. All in all, it's cheaper just to prevent your dog from getting sick in the first place.

ROCKY MOUNTAIN SPOTTED FEVER, ALSO KNOWN AS TICK BITE FEVER

The tick needs to be feeding on your dog for at least five to 20 hours for the parasite that causes tick bite fever to be transmitted. That's why you should check your dog immediately after a walk. Symptoms can start to show two days after the parasite enters the dog's system, but it can take up to two weeks to see the first signs. Some of the signs of this illness are:

- Loss of appetite
- Joint or muscle pain that can move around
- Fever
- Coughing
- Signs of other pain
- Swelling of the joints or of the face or legs
- Vomiting and diarrhea

Again, this is an illness that can be easily treated with antibiotics, but it is really important to get it treated quickly as it can lead to blood vessels dying and extremities becoming gangrenous. Severe cases can also lead to things like kidney disease and neurological disease. If the dog is very ill, such as if he is showing evidence of organ failure or isn't eating and is becoming dehydrated, he might need to be hospitalized.

HOW TO TELL IF YOUR DOG HAS FLEAS

With fleas, your Boerboel will scratch excessively. Fleas are easiest to spot in places on your Boerboel where he doesn't have as much hair. For example, the dog's stomach or the creases between the leg and body are spots where you can see fleas most easily.

Comb your dog with a flea comb. When you run your fingers or the flea comb in the opposite direction that your Boerboel's hair grows, that will part the hair, making it easier to spot the fleas. If you don't spot adult fleas, then you still might spot their droppings on the animal's skin. These are little round black pepper-like specks.

Some methods of prevention

Ticks and fleas can really make your dog sick, and there are a lot of options for treatments, such as one you use in the dog's bathwater, called a dip. This worked very well for our dogs, and we never had a problem. But if you have a dog with sensitive skin, this might not work for you.

Then, there are flea collars, but these can be carcinogenic to cats, and I have never found any of those to really work well with any of my Boerboels. I'm not sure whether it might be that they are too big for the collars to be effective.

Lastly, there are chewable tablets that keep your dog safe for up to 12 weeks. They don't generally affect your dog's skin or health, and they are really easy to use and effective. That said, this preventative is a bit more expensive than the other options.

Deworming

Even a really healthy and happy puppy can have worms. Normally, a puppy gets dewormed each time it's vaccinated. After that, he only really needs to be dewormed about once a year. But if you have a pup that likes to

Photo Courtesy
of Anna Linkman

chew on a lot of stuff outside or eat all sorts of things, then he may need to be dewormed every six months. Normally you can just buy an inexpensive chewable deworming tablet from your vet or supermarket. These deworming tablets treat the most common worms. But there are others, like those that are transmitted from mother to puppy, and those might require additional medical treatment.

ROUNDWORM

This is the most common gastrointestinal worm found in dogs. It can be transferred from a mother dog to her puppies through the placenta, but they can also get it from eating or sniffing feces from an infected dog. They can also be spread by rodents, earthworms, cockroaches, and birds. If your dog eats lots of creepy crawlies outside, it might be a good idea to deworm him regularly. Roundworm is most hazardous to puppies because it can affect their growth.

Signs that a pup has this type of worm can include a potbelly, stunted growth, and diarrhea. The vet will need to check the pup's feces under a microscope.

Treatment is fairly straightforward with prescribed medication, but a dog might need a number of treatments because some only kill the adult worms and not the larvae.

HOOKWORM

Hookworms actually attach themselves to the intestinal wall of the dog and then feed on his blood. When they lay eggs, hookworms eject them into the digestive tract, and they then pass into the environment through the dog's feces. These hatched eggs then grow and live in the soil, where they can penetrate a dog's skin just when he walks on it. Because they feed on your Boerboel's blood, hookworms can cause some serious issues, especially in puppies who might lose too much blood to survive. Older animals might show signs of weight loss and diarrhea.

The best way to prevent your Boerboel from getting hookworms is to deworm him and to keep your environment safe. That said, there are a number of treatments available.

TAPEWORM

A dog normally gets tapeworms from fleas that have tapeworm eggs; from animals such as birds, rabbits, and rodents; or from feces. When the dog ingests tapeworm eggs, they enter his digestive system, where they will continue to reproduce.

You can see the worms or dried pieces of them sticking on your dog's fur near the anus. The good news is that most dogs don't get sick from these worms, but they could lose weight. The vet will need a fecal sample in order to assess whether a dog is infected.

There are prescription drugs that are given orally or by injection. These dissolve the tapeworm right inside the intestine and don't result in a lot of side effects.

HEARTWORM

Heartworm is hard to prevent and can be lethal. Your dog can become infected when he gets bitten by a mosquito that has ingested the parasite. Then, it can take up to six months before your dog starts to get sick. These are the symptoms of heartworm:

- A persistent dry cough that seems to get worse when a dog exercises. This is because the parasite is moving into the lungs and creating blockages.
- A dog that is more tired than normal.
- Weight loss.
- Problems with breathing, maybe almost like an asthma attack.
- Protruding ribs because your dog's lungs may be filling up with water.
- Lungs that make strange noises.
- An enlarged liver, in the later stages of the infection.
- A heart murmur can also develop.

Treatment is long and expensive, and even then, there are no guarantees that your dog will be cured eventually. First, the vet will give your dog an injectable drug that kills the adult heartworms. Depending on how bad the dog's condition is, the vet will work out a schedule for these injections. Normally the vet will give one initial dose, then allow

HEALTH CHECK
Avoiding Ear Infections

Dogs with floppier ears like Boerboels can be prone to ear infections. Infections can happen when moisture gets trapped inside their ears, either from swimming, bathing, or just excessive humidity. Keeping your Boerboel's ears clean and dry can go a long way toward preventing infection. Ear infections can also be caused by underlying issues such as allergies or a tumor. If you suspect your Boerboel is suffering from an ear infection, don't hesitate to call the vet. If left untreated, ear infections can cause serious health issues for your dog.

for a 30-day resting period. Then two more injections will be given 24 hours apart. The dog will also be given antibiotics to make sure that no bacteria remain while the worms are dying.

The period of rest is absolutely vital. Keeping your dog completely quiet can be the difference between recovery and lifelong damage. During this time, the worms are dying and decomposing in your dog's body. They break up and travel to the dog's lungs. For weeks after treatment, these fragments of worms will still be inside the Boerboel's body. If your dog exercises, he could permanently damage his lungs or heart. Some vets recommend that you keep your dog in a crate most of the time following heartworm treatment to ensure that he does not overdo it.

Most dogs will have a cough during their treatment, but if it is really severe, then you need to inform your vet. Any other reactions need to be addressed quickly, too. If your dog shows loss of appetite; shortness of breath; severe coughing; a cough that is combined with blood; fever; or depression after being treated, get him to the vet right away. Reactions to the drugs don't happen often, but this is a severe illness with severe treatments, so be on the lookout.

Even after the adult heartworm is dead, heartworm larvae might remain in the dog. Because of this, either before or after treatment, your dog will be given another drug to kill the microfilariae. The vet needs to monitor the dog very closely after this medication is given, so they might keep your Boerboel in the hospital for the day.

While the treatment is ongoing, your Boerboel might need extra medication for the side effects. He might need pain relief drugs, a special diet to assist in recovery, diuretics to remove fluid in the lungs, etc. And even after all of that, you need to be prepared because it is possible that your Boerboel might need lifelong treatment against heart failure.

Treatment for heartworm is not easy on either your dog or yourself, but the good news is that it is treatable. While some side effects could remain, it is possible for a dog to have a long life after having heartworm.

Talk to your dog about preventive medications, which are far better than watching your dog suffer from the infection.

Holistic treatments

There are a lot of great holistic medical options available for canines, such as supplements that can help prevent certain illnesses. Acupuncture has been proven to help dogs with pain. It is an alternative medicine that comes from Chinese medicine, where small, thin needles are inserted into the skin to trigger an immune reaction and natural healing in the area.

Hydrotherapy is a great way to treat heavier dogs and help them lose weight. Hydrotherapy is a series of exercises that are done in warm water to help your dog build strength. This is because the dog's muscles work harder in water, but there is no resistance that can cause injury.

I would never recommend getting these treatments instead of vaccinating, but there are times they could be a good option. For example, if your dog gets a slight ear infection, it could be worth it to try something natural for a day or two before taking him to the vet. The danger lies in waiting too long and allowing an easily treatable condition to get so out of hand that your Boerboel suffers serious long-term damage.

The good news is that there are increasingly more vets who take a holistic approach. If that is important to you, I would advise finding a vet that is like-minded. That way, you ensure that your dog gets quality health care, and you can still have the peace of mind that the vet will use holistic treatments whenever possible.

Pet insurance

Vet care can be really expensive, and having pet insurance can literally be a lifesaver for your dog if he ever becomes seriously ill or gets into an accident. There are many times that a pet parent needs to make the excruciating decision whether or not to put a dog down or pay thousands to get the animal treated. Pet insurance can help you bridge the gap when you need it most.

There are many pet insurance options, each with its own customized plans. It will greatly depend on what you want out of your insurance. There are plans that only cover accidents and others that cover everything from vaccines and yearly check-ups to chronic illnesses. They each have a different price tag too. The more they cover, the more you are going to pay. But when you really need it, you will be grateful that you did get pet coverage.

CHAPTER 14

Boerboel-Specific Health Concerns

There are a few health-specific issues you'll need to look out for when it comes to your Boerboel.

Dangers of extreme temperatures

Boerboels were bred in Southern Africa. This means that Boerboels can deal with heat, but they struggle with very cold weather. Get your dog a jacket to wear when it is really cold. Top tip: some children's-size jerseys might be perfectly sized for your Boerboel.

When it is really cold, Boerboels need to be indoors in a warmer environment. If you live in a cold climate, and you don't want your Boerboel to come into the house, then you need to have a plan on how to get him inside a building when it is really cold. A dog kennel is not going to cut it.

Cancer

Sadly, I have lost quite a few of my Boerboels because of cancer. In older dogs, it can come on quite suddenly, and there isn't always time to get them properly treated.

When a younger dog gets cancer, it is much like when a human does. As long as you catch it early enough, there are often treatment options.

HEALTH CHECK
Boerboel Eye Disorders

Boerboels can be more prone to developing the eye disorders entropion or ectropion. Entropion is when the eyelid rolls in toward the eye, causing irritation. Ectropion is when the eyelid rolls outward. Both of these issues can lead to further complications, so it's best to discuss mitigation measures with your vet.

None of them are fun, but many of them can help your dog live a long and healthy life.

In older dogs, many vets don't want to treat cancer. The treatment can be really hard on them, and it might not help enough to warrant harsh treatments. The vet can give you medicine that can keep your dog comfortable and help him to stay healthy for as long as possible.

Two of my dogs got cancer in the joints of the legs. The only treatment for those dogs would have been to amputate their legs. And of course, for an older dog that can't adapt to such a serious change, it would just be cruel to put them through that.

Photo Courtesy of Tina and Ken Burgio

Things to look out for:

- Any strange bumps or lumps that you suddenly notice on your dog. They can grow over time, and you might not notice them at first so try to be as observant as possible.

- Any abnormal discharge from the eyes, ears, or rectum. It could be something treatable, so don't panic too quickly, but do get it checked out.

- Abdominal swelling. This is easier to spot when you don't have a dog that is a bit chubby—yet another reason to keep your dog's weight in check.

- Sores that just won't heal no matter what you do, or if the dog keeps getting sores and there is no reason for them.

- Sudden weight loss, especially if you are trying to get your dog to put on weight, and he just can't.

- Any abnormal odors that come from any part of the body. Dogs can smell at times, but if it's not a normal smell, or if you know the dog is really clean and he is suddenly smelly, then it can be a dangerous sign.

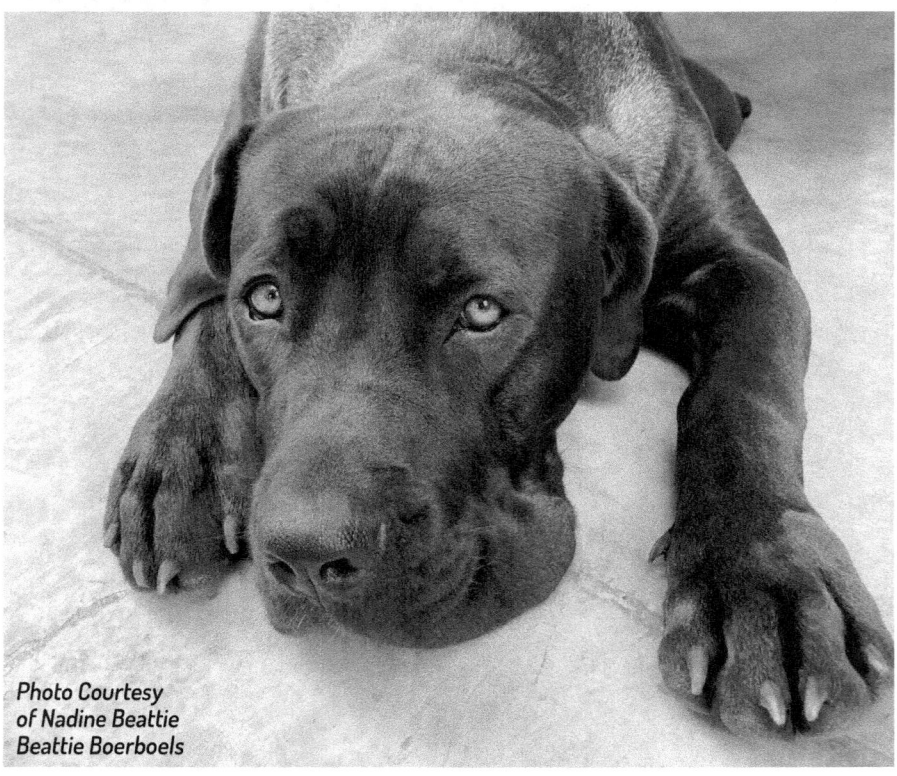

Photo Courtesy
of Nadine Beattie
Beattie Boerboels

If your dog suddenly has a change in appetite.

- Any difficulty breathing or coughing. Always get your dog checked if he is struggling to breathe.
- Changes in bathroom habits, such as pooping less often than before.
- If your dog is less active and seems really lethargic or depressed. Dogs slow down as they age anyway, but you will notice when it is unnatural. For example, when a dog who is obsessed with the ball just isn't interested in playing fetch, then you know there is a problem.
- Any evidence of pain. This needs to be checked out at all times too. You don't want your dog to suffer if you can help him.

Veterinary medicine has made incredible strides in treating cancer. The quicker you can get your dog diagnosed, the better the chances for a full recovery.

Hip and elbow dysplasia

In most big dogs, hip and elbow dysplasia can become a problem. This is when a dog's hip or elbow sockets have an abnormal growth with insufficient coverage of the bone, resulting in a joint that is loose or unstable. It can happen in a young pup, but normally you really start to notice a problem when your dog is around a year or two old. He can start to struggle with getting up. He may seem wobbly on his feet and not be able to run as easily as he used to. The good news is that dysplasia is treatable, and it shouldn't affect your dog's lifespan. The key thing here is to get help to manage your dog's pain.

Vets can treat the condition with surgery, but that can be pricey. Luckily, most pet insurance plans cover a big part of that sort of surgery. If there is a lot of damage, then the dog might still be in a bit of pain, but the vet can help you to keep that under control and ensure that your Boerboel has a life that is almost completely normal.

Skin disorders

Most Boerboels don't have major skin problems, but they can happen. If you notice that your Boerboel scratches a lot, especially if it is to the point of bleeding, then it is important to ensure there is no obvious reason for it, like ticks and fleas.

Most commonly, skin irritation in dogs can be an allergic reaction either to food or shampoo. Gradually change the dog's food—never change a dog's

Photo Courtesy
of Ekaterina Shimoliuk

food immediately, or that can upset its stomach—and give it a month or so. It takes a while for itchy skin related to food allergies to really completely disappear. If your dog is scratching himself seriously, you could get an oint-ment from the vet to put on the wounds.

If you see that the scratching gets worse each time that the dog has a bath, then it is important to get another brand or type of dog shampoo. Bathe him again with clean water without soap for a few weeks in order to completely get rid of any excess soap that can cause irritation on the skin.

Spinal problems

Most spinal injuries in Boerboels are caused by the cervical or thoracic vertebrae in the spine being malformed. I must stress, this is pretty rare. But sadly, it can happen.

Normally, spinal problems show up in the first two years of a dog's life as the animal grows and the spine stops being able to handle the weight. A wide variety of outcomes and treatments are possible, depending on the severity of the issue. Dogs with mild cases might only be prescribed pills like predni-sone, or no treatment may even be needed. The vet could decide to operate, or sadly, the issue could be so severe that they need to euthanize your pup.

The key thing is to make sure you get the dog to the vet as quickly as possible to ensure that he doesn't injure himself any further.

Things to look out for:

- Sudden shivering, especially if the pup doesn't want to get up or do anything in combination with this.
- The dog refuses to get up and play even if you offer enticement like a favorite toy or treat.
- Any signs of pain when you touch the dog.
- The dog can't bend down even for something simple like drinking water or eating.
- Your dog drags his back legs.
- It seems like your dog is not completely in control of the back half of his body.
- Any strange position that doesn't seem normal or comfortable. Dogs can lie in strange positions all the time, but this will look different from your dog just being an adorable weirdo. He might have an arched back or a pulled-in head and seem uncomfortable but unable to change the position.

- Any type of limping, especially if it doesn't go away after a few minutes.

If you see any such behavior, get your dog to the vet right away. Do not wait. This can be really serious.

Neurological issues

Again, this is not a type of disease that happens in Boerboels often, but it is possible. There are many different types of neurological issues, but most of them are really treatable.

Different types include:

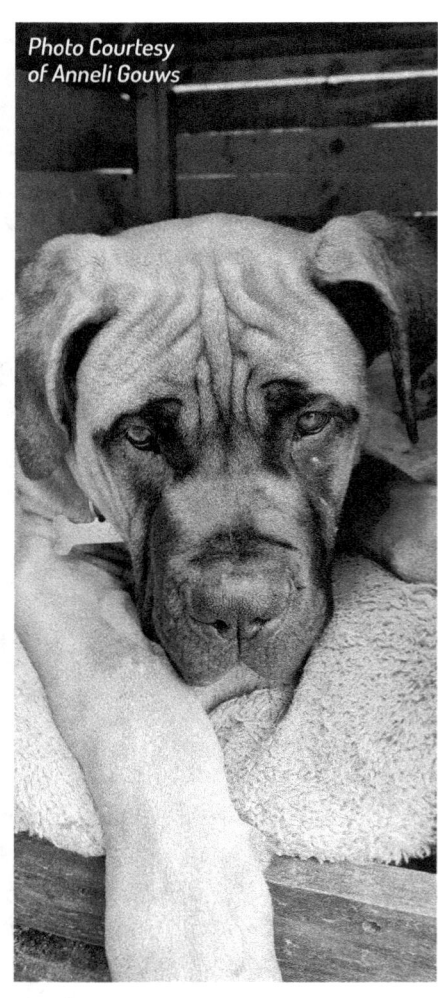

Photo Courtesy of Anneli Gouws

- Any autoimmune disease that can affect the brain or spinal cord. When the autoimmune disease is kept under control, the neurological issues will lessen.

- Inflammation that is somewhere along one of the components of the central nervous system. Once again, controlling the inflammation can mean that the neurological issue goes away too.

- Seizures. Some can be caused by epilepsy, some by disruptions in the system. I have never had a Boerboel with epilepsy, but my Yorkie does have it. It can look really scary, but it is very treatable.

- Strokes.

- Tumors of the nervous system.

Treatment plans will vary greatly depending on the problem that your Boerboel is facing, but the symptoms to look out for are pretty similar.

Things to look out for:

- Unexplained circling. Many dogs do this out of habit, but if your dog doesn't or he does it at a strange time or in a strange way, then it could be a symptom of a neurological problem.

- Pressing his head against something. There are a lot of cute photos on the internet of a dog pressing its head against a wall, but in reality, this can be a really dangerous sign. There might be pressure in the dog's head that he is trying to alleviate.

- Sudden weakness or if your dog suddenly stumbles repeatedly.

- Seizures.

- Pain. Pain is never a good thing and is always a reason to see a vet.

- Disorientation. If your dog looks like he is out of it or can't focus, it might be a symptom of a bigger issue.

- Losing the use of one or more limbs. A seizure may cause a dog to suddenly lose the use of his back legs. It's very scary, but it can be treated.

See a vet right away if a dog suddenly can't stand or if he keeps losing his balance and falling. There are many reasons this can happen, ranging from an ear infection to a brain inflammation. A sick dog can be really scary, and if you are anything like me, then you probably jump to the worst-case scenario right away. But when your dog is treated quickly, he has the best chance possible of making a full recovery.

CHAPTER 15

Travel with Your Boerboel

Traveling with any pet can be tricky, but when your baby is a 200-pound beast, then it can be just a little bit harder...but it is possible. It is also good to plan ahead for the times that your Boerboel isn't able to travel with you.

Getting your Boerboel used to car rides

The best time to get your Boerboel used to car rides is when he's a puppy. Full disclosure: when your Boerboel is fully grown, he will probably take up most of the back seat, so don't plan on taking many other passengers.

Having the heating or air conditioning on in a car can help to keep your Boerboel comfortable, but they can also dehydrate a dog. Make sure that

Photo Courtesy of Monica Sciocatti

Photo Courtesy
of Odeta Turkuvienė

you regularly stop to give your dog water. Alternatively, you can take snacks like pieces of apple to keep your dog hydrated during the trip.

There are dog seat belts that allow your dog to be able to move around but still be safe. Seat belts also help to ensure that your dog can't just climb over the seat and sit on your lap. If you have a vehicle that is big enough, and if you have crate trained your dog, that might be the best safety strategy. The crate will already be the dog's happy place, and it will help him relax.

If you have a normal-sized car, then a Boerboel can easily learn how to get in and out of the car on his own. Open the car, show your dog a treat, and give the command to get in. Then, possibly place the treat on the seat. When he is a puppy, you can give him a little push and help him. Eventually, he will just get in on command.

If you own a higher vehicle, such as a truck, then you might need to teach your dog how to get in with the help of a dog ramp, using the same strategy as for a normal-sized car. It is really crucial to teach your dog how to get in the car on his own since there will come a time that lifting him in is not going to be so easy for you. It will spare you a lot of effort and back pain.

Dogs are prone to getting car sick, but when a pup gets used to traveling in a car, and the ride is made enjoyable, then his car sickness will usually become less too. Sadly, some dogs will just never stop getting car sick, and no amount of getting used to it will help. In the case of such dogs, you can get a tablet that helps your dog to relax and that alleviates car sickness.

When going on a road trip, make sure that you stop frequently and allow your Boerboel to stretch his legs and potty as needed. Give him plenty of fluids to ensure that he stays hydrated. Take some favorite toys and blankets to comfort him.

It is really important to never, ever leave your dog alone in the car, especially not in extreme weather.

Is it possible to take your Boerboel on long trips?

Yes, it is possible. But it is going to take a lot of planning and extra care. First, if you are going to go out of state, you need to check the legalities surrounding Boerboels in the state you are visiting. To remind yourself of some of the legal issues around the Boerboel, reread chapter 1 of this book.

Then you need to find accommodations that are willing to allow you to bring a 200-pound dog with you. Such places do exist, but you will need to make an effort to find them.

HOTELS AND OTHER ACCOMMODATION

It might be possible to find a house that you can rent or an Airbnb that does allow animals and possibly even really large dogs. Somewhere that has

Photo Courtesy of Jason Jess

a garden for your dog to relax in could be best. It is possible to find some hotels that will allow it too. But be prepared. Chances are that with such a large dog, the housing fees could be really steep. Or they could just charge a deposit to ensure that your dog doesn't destroy anything.

FUN FACT
Breed Popularity

Boerboels were only recently recognized by the American Kennel Club (AKC), being admitted to the AKC Working Group in 2015. As of 2021, Boerboels are ranked as 121st most popular out of 200 breeds.

Do a Google search specifically for dog-friendly hotels in the area where you are visiting. Then call to ask if they are comfortable with allowing a dog that is as big as a Boerboel to stay at their hotel. Ask for any specific fees or requirements, such as muzzling or crating. Be willing to compromise.

ON FLIGHTS

Flying with your dog is also a possibility, but that opportunity becomes increasingly slim as your dog grows up. There are some airlines that will allow a Boerboel to travel, but the requirements are regularly changing. Check them before making a booking. Even between flights, there are sometimes new requirements you need to adhere to. One requirement that is consistent among all airlines is that any dog traveling in the cargo hold must be in an IATA-approved kennel. This ensures there is enough room for your Boerboel to stand up, turn around, and lie down.

Normally, airlines require your dog's vaccinations to be completely up to date, and a dog as big as a Boerboel will normally only be allowed in the luggage compartment. That means you will need to put him in a strong crate. You will have to take him to the luggage area and drop him off until after the flight when you can once again retrieve him as luggage. Most airlines ask that you attach two bowls on top of the crate, one they can fill with water and one that they will fill with ice. Dogs don't need to eat during the flight (in fact, it's better if they don't) and should also skip the meal immediately prior to the flight. This will help them avoid getting sick due to stress and an upset stomach.

Find out as many details as possible before the flight and make sure that you are happy with the arrangements. It can be stressful for both you and the Boerboel to travel, so making sure you know exactly what to expect is important and will make it as easy as possible.

The cost of traveling with a dog as big as a Boerboel can be pretty steep. It can cost anywhere from $200 all the way up to $1000. This price normally goes up with the size of the dog. For a Boerboel, expect to pay more toward the higher end of the range.

OTHER THINGS TO CONSIDER

Lastly, you will need to check out every place that you are going to visit to make sure that your Boerboel is allowed to come with you. Leaving your Boerboel at the hotel might not be feasible, so check out everything from dog-friendly restaurants to parks where big dogs are allowed to visit. Don't travel and hit snags because of poor planning.

Dog sitters vs. kennels

Both these options have merits and drawbacks. In the end, you are going to rely greatly on what you and your Boerboel are comfortable with. The biggest key is to get him comfortable with your chosen option as young as you possibly can.

Dog sitters

A dog sitter is a great option if you have someone that you can completely rely on and who knows your dog really well. If you find someone who is reliable, it can be a wonderful experience.

Dog sitters, especially those that stay in your house and care for your dog there, give a pup the added bonus of being in his own safe home environment. But you need to make sure that you trust the sitter with your dog and home completely. There have sadly been cases where the pet parents got home, and the dog had been really neglected. Trying it for a short stay at first might be the best option.

If you feel more comfortable checking in on your dog via video call and seeing in real-time that he is taken care of and fed, that is completely within your rights. Do not be afraid of setting that as one of the terms of the dog sitting agreement.

Dog sitters will take your dog for a daily walk while you are gone, feed him, and many will stay with them in your home. If you use a regular dog walking service, then it might be a great place to find a dog sitter that already knows your dog and that your dog is comfortable with. If you get a dog sitter that stays in your home, the person will do dual duty taking care of your dog and your home, too, watering your plants and bringing in the mail. That said, they might ask for an additional fee for house sitting.

Just remember, you need a pet sitter with experience with big dogs who won't be scared of your pup when you aren't around.

Kennels

Kennels or dog hotels can be really great or really bad. The bonus of these places is that you can tour the facility and check it out before leaving your precious pup in their care. If you aren't allowed to do so, that is a massive red flag, and I would seriously reconsider leaving your Boerboel there.

There are different types of kennels available. Some specialize in smaller dogs and some in larger dogs. Make sure you know where your dog will be kept. Some places keep small dogs inside and big dogs in kennels outside. Make sure you are comfortable with the arrangements and that it is what your dog is used to. There is nothing worse than coming back and finding a severely traumatized pup.

There are also many kennels that are more luxurious than some hotel rooms. There are kennels that have televisions and heating or air conditioning in the rooms. Some kennels provide walks and playtime with other dogs and will take care of your dog more than you probably do yourself.

Some provide the same diet as you give your dog at home or allow you to provide your dog's food for kennel staff to feed him.

Most kennels will require you to get your dog checked to ensure he is healthy before he stays with them. This protects both your dog and other dogs in the kennel.

Separation anxiety

This can be a hard one because Boerboels are not called Velcro dogs for no reason. They like to stick with you, and they do get separation anxiety. For many of us, the answer to that is normally to make more of a fuss and start stressing out when we need to leave. This is the exact opposite of what you should be doing with a dog with separation anxiety.

Don't punish your dog. It is not his fault. He just loves you. But the best way to handle separation anxiety is to largely ignore it.

- Come and go often. Have your dog stay outside or in one room while you go to another. Again, this is not for punishment. Do not speak to your dog harshly when he tries to follow. Just close the door.

Photo Courtesy of Hilary Calton

- Ignore him. This is really hard on any animal lover. But if the anxiety is so severe that the dog won't eat or he harms himself when you are gone, then you might need to take drastic steps. Ignore him for a week or two when you are home. Have someone else take him for walks, feed him, and play with him. Get him to see that you can't be his entire world.

- And if you really need to, get the help of a behavioral specialist.

Moving

Moving homes is stressful not only for you but for your animals too. The disruption in their surroundings and routines can be brutal, so make sure that you give them a lot of attention and care when you move.

If you are still packing at the old house, keep the dog with you. If you take things to the new house and are going to start unpacking there and be there more of the time, take him over there too. Don't be afraid to ask the vet to give you something to relax your dog if he is high strung, and make sure to give him a lot of attention in his new surroundings. Dog proof the new home before you go and set up a little corner for him to relax in with his own belongings as soon as possible.

CHAPTER 16

When Your Pup Becomes a Senior

A senior dog can still be just as loving as a puppy, sometimes even more so, as you have been with him his entire life. It can be said that when you adopt a puppy, you know he will break your heart in about 10 years or so. But it is still worth every second. In this chapter, we will deal with the challenges of a senior dog and what to expect when it is time to say goodbye.

Life expectancy of a Boerboel

> "Hopefully you will have an older Boerboel. They are worth their weight in gold. You can't go wrong with using joint supplements to keep your dog comfortable and moving well. Keep him at a healthy weight with as much movement as he wants. Learn to watch and enjoy his long, snore-filled naps!"
>
> KATE NICHOLSON
> Wilby Boerboels

As with all bigger dogs, the Boerboel's life expectancy is much shorter than that of a smaller-breed dog. In my experience, bigger Boerboels tend to die younger than smaller Boerboels do.

Boerboels have a life expectancy of 10 to 12 years. Large and giant-breed dogs like the Boerboel are already considered senior dogs from around the age of six to seven years old. Of course, just like with humans, a dog's life expectancy can be greatly impacted by a number of factors, like exercise levels, weight, and general health.

The signs of aging for your Boerboel include:

- Muscle loss; your dog might seem smaller than he used to.

- Weight fluctuations; some dogs lose weight because they don't want to eat as much; others pick up weight because their activity decreases.

- Your dog's eyes might seem a bit duller than before; this is because there is a thickening of the lens over time.

- Different sleeping habits. Some dogs sleep more because they are tired; others have trouble finding a comfortable spot to sleep in.

- Dementia. Yes, even dogs get it. If you see your senior baby staring at walls or blankly into space, it might be because of this.

- Hearing loss.

- Trouble with gums and teeth falling out.

- Graying hairs, especially around the muzzle and face.

Photo Courtesy of Lynn and Wade Walcott

Basic care for senior Boerboels

The biggest golden rule for looking after a senior dog is just to love him. He might not be able to jump up and down from the excitement of seeing you anymore; he might not be able to run with you in the park, but he still loves you just as fiercely as he ever did. You are still his entire world. And as the time starts to become shorter, you need to make sure that time is filled with as much love and care as you can possibly give this dog that is still your baby.

Seniors still need exercise, but they might not be able to go for long walks. Take your dog on shorter walks and keep to your dog's speed. Running might be out at this stage.

Take your dog for regular check-ups to make sure that you spot any disease quickly.

Give your dog proper nutrition. At an older age, it is more important than ever to ensure that your dog does not become obese. Give him food for senior dogs. Those foods normally include extra vitamins and minerals that can help your aging Boerboel. Senior dogs have fewer calories per cup than adult or puppy food, and they have fewer proteins and fats than food for younger dogs. They also have higher carbohydrates than diets of adults or puppies. This works better for a dog that sleeps more and is less active.

Play with your dog. Just because a dog is old does not mean he doesn't want to play anymore. It might just mean that the playtime will be shorter, and he might need more naps.

What to expect of your aging Boerboel

"

"We have had several Boerboels who have made it to 12 and 14 years of age. As they age, it's important to make things easier for them. Give your dog lots of cushions to lie on, and try to avoid going up and down stairs too often. Putting an old dog on vitamin and joint supplements to keep his old bones comfy and to ensure he gets all the nutrients he needs is a must."

MICHELLE CONVIS
Adara Ridge Boerboels

"

*Photo Courtesy
of Irene Krohn*

This is still the same dog that you have loved since he was a bouncy puppy. His personality won't change. He might just get slower, and he might not be able to react to your every command, mostly because he doesn't hear you, but he will still be there for you.

A number of issues, like incontinence, hearing loss, or tooth loss, might come your way. Now is the time to repay your dog for all the years of being your loyal friend. It is horrible to see how many dogs are dropped off at shelters yearly for the crime of becoming old. Please never do that to your dog.

You might need to be a little more patient, but there are ways to deal with these issues. Get advice and allow them to live out his golden years in the place that he is most happy, right by your side.

Issues senior dogs can face include:

ARTHRITIS

We have spoken about this in previous sections, but the problem can become bigger as a dog ages, especially a dog as large as a Boerboel. Joint pain can be a big indication of arthritis, but dogs don't have to be in constant pain. There are lots of treatments for painful conditions and painkillers that the vet can prescribe that can really help a dog's quality of life and keep him happy and comfortable. Please see chapter 13 for more information on arthritis.

DEMENTIA

Dementia is a sad part of aging that can occur in any breed, but with a lot of patience and love, your dog can still have a happy life. Make sure he can always find his food and water and stick to a routine where possible to help the dog adapt and cope. Make sure that he can't get out and wander off, but still give him plenty of exercise. Keep him mentally stimulated with things like a ball that releases snacks.

It might get to a stage where the dog will need to be with someone most of the time. Sadly, at some stage, the dog's quality of life might become so compromised that you will have to make the hard decision to let him go for his own good. Some symptoms of dog dementia include:

- Trouble sleeping
- General anxious behavior
- Being more vocal than normal and at inappropriate times, like howling or whining
- Repetitive behavior like a dog that paces back and forth
- Staring at walls
- Not being as social as he normally is
- Getting disoriented, even in a place that the dog is familiar with

BLINDNESS

Dogs that get older can start to lose their sight. It can be hard to deal with when your once playful puppy starts to have difficulties. It is not something that you can really change, but you can make life easier for your dog. Softly speaking to him before you touch him will help so that you don't startle your dog. Make sure that everything in the house stays the same. Each time you rearrange the furniture, it will make it harder for the dog to maneuver.

There are some types of eye illnesses that can be reversed, like cataracts that can cause blindness. Some of the symptoms of this are cloudy eyes and your dog constantly rubbing his eyes. Cataract surgery is very successful. It breaks up the cloudy lens in front of the eyes, helping a dog to see again.

DEAFNESS

Senior dogs can start to lose their hearing. Their recall will obviously be harder because they won't be able to hear when you call them. Even a dog that used to be completely fine going for off-leash walks should be kept leashed at this stage for his own safety. But there are ways to still speak to your Boerboel. Teaching a dog hand signals at a younger age will help when they can't hear a verbal command. You will also need to be more careful when you are driving your car into your driveway. A dog that has gone deaf will have less warning when it comes to danger. You will need to become his ears.

Photo Courtesy of Wendy Lehr

INCONTINENCE

This can be another big problem in older dogs. But once again, there are things you can do to make it easier on your dog. Make sure to take your dog out more frequently than you would have in the past. At night, there are potty pads that are large enough to place on the dog bed or wherever your dog sleeps. There are even dog nappies that come in large sizes to keep your dog comfortable and your house clean.

LOSING TEETH

Your senior dog could lose his teeth, too, and if that is the case, you will need to adapt his diet so he can eat without having difficulty. Softer foods will be best at this stage.

QUALITY OF LIFE

For most of these things, you need to consider your dog's quality of life to try and understand when you are keeping him alive for your own benefit and when it is time to let them go. It all depends on your dog's daily lifestyle and if the good still outweighs the bad.

Some factors to consider when looking at quality of life are:

- **Pain** – This depends on whether or not you can keep your dog's pain levels in check. If he isn't breathing well or is constantly whining or crying, even when on pain medication, then it is a good indication that his pain is not in control.

- **Mobility** – A dog might not want to walk as much, but if he can still move when he needs to, he still has some quality of life. If you need to carry him everywhere, that might be an indication that his quality of life is not great.

- **Breathing issues** – When a dog can't eat or drink because of breathing issues, that's an indicator of poor life quality.

- **Hygiene issues** – If you need to help your dog to go potty, such as taking him out more often than before, that could be fine. But when it comes to the point that he lies in his own feces or urine, that is an issue.

- **Eating or drinking** – If your dog can still eat and drink, even in smaller portions and slower than normal, that's fine. But if he can't eat or drink at all, that's an issue.

- **Social interactions** – If he is still a relatively happy dog that wants to be with you, then he has a good quality of life, even if things can be hard. But if he doesn't want to spend time with you or won't let you touch him, then it could be a sign of a very sick dog.

- **More good days than bad** – Toward the end of your dog's life, there are going to be some harder days, but when there are still a lot more good ones than bad, that is a good indication your dog still has a relatively good quality of life.

Loving them until the end

The hardest day in any animal lover's world is the day they need to say goodbye. And there are so many ways that it can go that it is never really possible to completely prepare for it.

I have lost dogs in so many different ways. There have been those that went to take a nap and then never woke up. Those that became so sick that I had to make the incredibly heartbreaking decision to let them go. Those that I cared for all through the night because the vet wasn't open, only to lose them an hour before the clinic opened. The one thing they all have in common is how much they hurt and how much it is going to rip your heart to shreds, and that in itself is a thing of beauty. It shows the incredible bond that we can have with an animal.

Dogs have a way of allowing you to realize that it is time. If they don't have a good quality of life, then the kindest thing for you to do might be to let them go.

Before you call the vet, you might want to spend a bit of time with your dog. Allow family members or close friends the opportunity to say a proper goodbye. This is not always possible, so when it is, then it is a good opportunity to make the moment as joyful as possible.

Allow your dog to do some of his favorite things where possible. Give him some of his favorite snacks, or possibly even those that he could never have, like chocolate. Just spend a few hours of really good quality time together. Soak up these last memories and give your pup another great day surrounded by the people he loves the most.

You may decide to get a mobile vet to come and euthanize your dog at your home, where he is comfortable, or you may take him to the vet. Both have pros and cons. At home, it will be a less stressful environment for both of you. Your dog can go to sleep in the same place where he was happy. But it can also be a traumatic moment for you, and if the procedure is performed at home, there can be a constant reminder.

At the vet, they have everything planned out already, and they can make it easier for you. But it can be stressful for you and your dog to go to a strange place and say goodbye there. At the same time, they have the means to dispose of your dog's body easier, and it can be less traumatic than having him at home and needing to take care of his remains yourself.

If you have small children, now is also a good time to decide if you want them to be around when your dog is being euthanized. You could allow it as a way of giving them closure, but you could also decide that they should say goodbye beforehand. There are no easy answers to this question, and it will be completely up to you and what you think is best for your child.

THE PROCESS OF EUTHANASIA

Before even starting the process, I suggest that you handle any paperwork and arrangements; then that is one less thing that you need to worry about after everything is done. Planning ahead can make it much easier on you in the most difficult moments.

The vet will connect an IV line and give your dog medicine. The medicine they most often use is a seizure drug that they essentially give in an overdose quantity. It renders your Boerboel unconscious almost right away and stops heart and brain functions soon after. The process normally takes less than two minutes and is almost completely painless, aside from the brief needle

sting when they put in the IV. The liquid medicine can be thick and colored, normally a purple color. It can all feel very overwhelming, but because the medicine has sedative qualities, know that your pet is not in pain.

Then the vet will allow you to say goodbye and comfort your dog while they inject the medicine that will stop his vital signs. This is normally a gentle transition, like your dog is falling asleep. He might twitch or spasm. He might urinate or defecate, and you might see him take a final breath. Don't be alarmed; none of this is an indication of pain.

Stay by your dog's side, as he has always been by yours, until the moment that he goes. Speak to him softly. Cuddle him, give him scratches, and just love him. It will make one of the hardest moments in both your lives just a bit more bearable.

Your dog will eventually stop breathing, and then he will be gone. The vet will check his vital signs at this stage and let you know that it is over.

Vets try to make it as easy on pet parents as they possibly can. They know how much you are hurting at that stage.

CHOOSING WHAT TO DO AFTER

Afterward, you will have to decide what to do with your dog's body. This decision is really hard, and it might be easier to make it before the time comes since your emotions will be fragile at that stage, and you will be hurting. When you see that the time is getting closer, you might want to look into your options.

BURYING

Some people want to bury their dog in the garden, but with a dog that is Boerboel size, this isn't entirely practical. And in many states, it is illegal too. Look into the practicalities and legalities in your state.

CREMATION

FUN FACT
Oldest Boerboel Bloodline

The Ysterberg Mastiff is considered to be the oldest Boerboel bloodline, dating back to the 1940s. These early Boerboels existed before the breed was formally recognized and were bred by Klaas van Waveren in South Africa. Opinions are divided on whether Ysterbergs were their own separate breed and part of the foundation stock for Boerboels or whether Ysterbergs are similar enough to Boerboels to be considered the same.

Just like with human cremations, there are different options to choose from, such as having your dog cremated on his own (a more expensive option) and then receiving his ashes. If you have your dog cremated with other animals, this is a less expensive option. It depends on what you feel is right and on what will give you the best closure.

PET CEMETERIES

The vet could put you in contact with a pet cemetery where they can bury your dog. You could also get a pet memorial, such as a park bench.

The end of your journey together is never going to be easy, and you will probably never be completely prepared for it. But you will be able to have a little bit of comfort in the fact that your Boerboel was loved, that you gave him a wonderful life, and he loved you until the end.